LONG SCHOTT

Building Homes, Dreams, and Baseball Teams

Steve Schott

with John Shea

TRIUMPH
BOOKS

No part of this publication may be reproduced, stored in a retrieval system, or transmitted in any form by any means, electronic, mechanical, photocopying, or otherwise, without the prior written permission of the publisher, Triumph Books LLC, 814 North Franklin Street, Chicago, Illinois 60610.

Library of Congress Cataloging-in-Publication Data available upon request.

This book is available in quantity at special discounts for your group or organization. For further information, contact:

Triumph Books LLC
814 North Franklin Street
Chicago, Illinois 60610
(312) 337-0747
www.triumphbooks.com

Printed in U.S.A.
ISBN: 978-1-62937-977-7
Design by Patricia Frey

All photos courtesy of the author.

To my grandchildren, who will learn what it takes to find the road to success, happiness, and peace with God, themselves, and their families.

—S.S.

In memory of Sam Spear, a great friend who helped initiate this project and whose generous and vibrant spirit will remain forever.

—J.S.

Contents

Foreword

WHEN BILLY BEANE FIRST OFFERED ME the assistant general manager job with the Oakland A's, I didn't even think to ask for a chance to meet the ownership. I was so excited that it didn't cross my mind, but really, I had no idea how critical ownership was to any successful sports franchise.

All sports team owners want to win, and while nearly all of them wouldn't mind losing a few dollars to help make that happen, none of them enthusiastically lose millions without the accompanying ring. That makes life interesting for the general manager, as the best job security for a GM is winning games. So what do typical GMs want to do? Spend as much as possible to help them win. After all, it's not their money. This creates a culture in which the GM is constantly asking ownership for more money, making the case that the extra spend will get them that much closer to the coveted championship. This dynamic prompted one MLB owner to proclaim that every organization's biggest enemy is his own general manager.

The Oakland A's under Steve Schott were different. Yes, Steve wanted to win as badly as any other owner, even though our team didn't generate the same revenue as our competitors. However, he also was shrewd enough to know that if we tried to spend an extra $1 million on players to gain an edge, our competitors would react by spending $2 million. If we tried to spend an extra $5 million, they would just spend $10 million.

Steve imparted to us that this particular strategy is a foolish way to attempt to compete, whether with a baseball team or in any other venture, as you end up losing both on and off the field. That made a lasting impression on Billy and me, and I think that's still the way the A's think about the world long after Steve's ownership.

And rightfully so. Steve created a framework in Oakland that was the foundation for our success. First, he created our operating box, containing two goals: the first was to win as many games as possible, and the second was not to lose money. That wasn't necessarily a novel concept, but the clarity of the dual goals was key.

Second, which was both unusual and absolutely essential, Steve granted us complete autonomy to operate within that box. That may not seem like that big a deal, but imagine for a second that you just purchased a professional sports franchise for hundreds of millions of dollars, and rather than getting involved with the player decisions, you instead tell your operators that they have total autonomy. Who does that?

What Steve knew then, and what we realized only later, was that by providing us with both restrictions and autonomy, he was teaching us how to think like owners. We couldn't run to him saying, "We need some money to sign a left-handed reliever," because sometimes when you give people too many resources, they get sloppy and wasteful. Instead, we just had to figure it out. Want to hire additional staff? Figure it out. Need new software? Figure it out. Want another bat off the bench? Figure it out. Every off-season, we would wipe the board clean and start with a payroll that wouldn't lose money. That was our box. Rather than staring at our roster and thinking that we needed another outfielder or starting pitcher, we had to think much more broadly about how to create a competitive organization within that box. That completely changed our mentality, and without that disciplined construct he created for us, there's really no way we would have done some of the things we did in Oakland.

Third, as long as we maintained our discipline, Steve was willing to live with mistakes. Consequently, we tried all sorts of different things, big and small. He wasn't hanging over our shoulders and criticizing every decision that didn't work—and there were plenty of them! It's not as though Steve never had input or didn't have constructive comments, but he trusted us to think like owners, and we took that responsibility personally. While the restrictions of our construct forced us to think differently about how we were going to build a competitive team, it also gave us a creative license to try to make it happen. When faced with a difficult decision, people would tell us all the time, "You have to do this, or you have to do that." Billy would respond, "We're Oakland. We don't *have* to do anything." When people feel safe enough in their environment to say what they really think, to push boundaries and to experiment, it's called "psychological safety." That wasn't a hot term in the late 1990s, but we had it. In fact, Steve created that for us long before I arrived in Oakland.

If you were to open the Oakland A's media guide late in 1998 when I joined the organization, you'd have seen that it was this person's 15th year with the A's, that person's 18th year, another person's 22nd year. It was unbelievable. That stability just doesn't exist in professional sports. Steve Vucinich, Mickey Morabito, Keith Liepmann, J.P. Ricciardi, Larry Davis, Pam Pitts, Ted Polakowski, Dick Bogard, Grady Fuson, and more. Usually an owner buys a team, comes in, and wipes everything out, but Steve didn't do that. He stayed with Sandy Alderson, stayed with Billy, and allowed virtually the entire baseball operation to continue to do its job. That was Steve's first step in creating that foundation of psychological safety.

From there, Sandy's culture of being inquisitive, thoughtful, and ethical continued to grow, and then Billy built on that with his energy, iron will, and growth mindset. It was all part of the recipe that Steve made possible.

When we were going through the Moneyball years in Oakland, before the book or the movie, we had no perspective on what it might mean. We were just trying to win. That's it. We were trying to win every day, every week, every month, every year, constantly looking for any edge and relishing the underdog role. When I look back at it now and process the special accomplishments and the lessons learned, I think all of us feel incredibly lucky to have been just a small part of it.

Similarly, since leaving Oakland more than 17 years ago, I've been with more teams in Major League Baseball, moved to the NFL, and also worked outside of sports, so I can put Steve's ownership in better perspective now than I could back then. Steve was passionate, supercompetitive, and proud of our teams, and at the end of the year when we lost in the playoffs, he was just as upset as everybody else. The fact that we had a low payroll didn't factor into his thinking; he never used it or allowed us to use it as an excuse.

I think back to a conversation Billy must have had with Steve—"Hey, Steve, we've got a great idea. We're going to sign Scott Hatteberg to play first base to replace the American League MVP, Jason Giambi, even though he's never played the position and hit .245 with three homers last year"—and, well, I can't help but laugh. Most owners probably would look at you cross-eyed, but not Steve.

As a decision maker, you can't ask for anything more than a clearly defined operating framework combined with autonomy and psychological safety: "These are your boundaries. Go get it. Don't be afraid to fail." It may sound simple, but it takes a special owner to create that environment—Moneyball would not have happened without it. I look back and relish those years in Oakland. I had no idea how good we had it.

—Paul DePodesta

Preface

FOR ME, THE BEST THING ABOUT MAKING MONEY is giving it away.

Growing up a few blocks from a college campus, I was fortunate to take advantage of the facilities. It was my neighborhood playground. Kids would walk over there, play basketball in the gym, and go for a dip in the pool, if a priest was around to let them in. There was no Little League, no youth leagues, nothing organized for kids. We figured it out on our own. There weren't many cars back then, and we played out in the street or walked over to the college. We didn't know any better at the time, but both the gym and the pool would be condemned today. Over time, they were replaced and upgraded but were never in line with other universities.

After high school, I was fortunate to get a baseball scholarship to that same college, Santa Clara University—a wonderful opportunity to receive a good college education. I was a pitcher in high school, and the college coach thought enough of me to offer a scholarship. I felt it was a lot of money, a big investment in me. It was a partial scholarship, which basically paid the tuition. You'll laugh at what tuition cost back then. It was $325 a semester, $650 a year. But to me, that was a ton of money. I appreciated it, and I felt indebted and wanted to pay it back. I felt it was incumbent on me to give back. That was always my desire.

Through the years, I never lost that desire, though I didn't have much money to give back at first. I was making $500, $600 a month, then a thousand a month and up to $16,000 to $18,000 a year by my late 30s. With three kids and a house payment. I wasn't making a lot, so I couldn't give much away. A few bucks here, a few bucks there, whatever I could give. In those days, I knew I wanted to make a lot of money, but I never imagined going on to own a home-building company or a baseball team, the Oakland A's.

My father was a city engineer, a public servant, a smart man with a very important job but one that paid hardly any money in those days. My mom was thrifty as can be, but it's not as if my brother, sister, and I had to worry about our next meal. When I received that scholarship, it gave me an opportunity to go to a school I never could have afforded without that financial help, and it meant everything to me.

Giving back always made me feel good, always seemed the right thing to do. If a college was going to pay my tuition and allow me the pleasure of playing on its baseball team for four years, I wasn't going to forget it, and I didn't. When I started making more money, I started giving back more.

That was the start of it: giving back to the university. I started donating to charities and schools and churches and groups and individuals, and the feeling always was the same. I got more of a thrill giving it away than making it. Money is a wonderful thing if you use it in the right ways.

One issue I had when I decided to write this book was that I'm not all that comfortable talking about myself. I didn't want it to be all about me. It wasn't about pumping my ego. I didn't need or want that. It's the same reason I don't have my name on the title of my company. I wanted this book to be interesting and, in some cases, lighthearted and maybe get some laughs from readers. And I wanted it to be more about sharing stories and ideas and explaining some of my successes— and failures—especially in business. I want it to help younger people coming up, including my grandchildren and their children and anyone else who might be interested in how a guy who had no money as a kid played baseball in college, got married at age 23—Pat and I had $500 between us in our pockets—and was fortunate to become financially successful enough to run my own company as well as own the A's during a special time in the organization's history.

We made four straight trips to the playoffs in the early 2000s but kept losing in the first round. It still was a great run with terrific players, a lot of hardworking people behind the scenes, and countless memorable moments—some highlighted in the *Moneyball* book and movie, but many not.

The A's were always the underdogs, never the favorites. But we strived to achieve. Being the underdog raises the bar for you. The outside world doesn't expect anything of you. We got more with less, and we were successful getting more with less. It was a true team effort on and off the field.

It was similar in business. My company didn't always have a big name. We were privately owned and up against some big competition with big bankrolls—the Yankees of homebuilding—and we had to work extra hard. We didn't have money to burn like a lot of these companies. Like with the A's, everybody worked together to accomplish a lot of goals.

I've been giving money away for 40-plus years, and about the time I bought into the A's in 1995, we formed our foundation, the Stephen C. & Patricia A. Schott Foundation. It is a bigger forum for us to support hundreds of charities, institutions, and causes, most involving education: grammar schools, high schools, scholarship funds, educational funds, and a lot of other ventures, including Santa Clara University, where the origin of the giving-back idea began.

Part One

MY ROOTS

Chapter 1

A Spiritual Upbringing

IT WAS 2003, AND THE OAKLAND A'S were in Boston to face the Red Sox in the American League Championship Series. Our team hotel was a short walk from the St. Francis Chapel in the Prudential Center, so I was able to go to mass before Game 3 along with a group from our traveling party. Everything was OK until the final blessing, when the priest said, "Let's say a prayer for the Red Sox."

From the congregation, I spoke up and said, "We're A's fans. We're with the A's organization." I didn't say I was the owner, but the priest was somewhat embarrassed. I probably shouldn't have spoken up. He said, "Oh, we don't want to overlook the visiting team. We can say a prayer for the A's." I had to laugh. But it wasn't so funny in the end. We came to Boston with a two-games-to-none lead, dropped both games at Fenway Park, and got eliminated in a Game 5 loss back in Oakland.

My mother, Mary, believed in Catholic schools and education, and instilled religion in me. My father, Edgar, was religious but not like my mom. She had a big impact on me. She cracked the whip, and we followed her. Attended mass every Sunday, *every day* during Lent. I was an altar boy all the way through eighth grade and had to learn the mass in Latin. It wasn't easy. The priest would start the prayer, and we had to finish it. When I got older, I continued going to mass even when I was playing Sunday ballgames. I'd work it out. I attended a seminary my freshman year in high school before moving over to Bellarmine College Prep in San Jose, but people thought it was my brother, Larry, who'd be a priest. He was very spiritual. He decided against it and later got married. My sister Dianne's son, Mark, did become a priest, and I think much of the inspiration came from my sister and his maternal grandmother, Mary Schott.

> *"I have so many peers who feel the world owes them a living. Don't be like that. Don't be like the grasshopper from 'The Ant and the Grasshopper.' You can't help but feel better if you can make others feel better. The greatest word in the English language is 'empathy.' It costs so little to do, but it makes such a big difference."*
> —Mary Schott

One year, my wife, Pat, and I were fortunate enough to visit the Vatican and Pope John Paul II. A very special experience. He was all in white and looking good. At the foot of the altar, he bowed and said a few words. He spoke English OK and said, "Stephen and Patricia, God bless you," and gave his blessing. It was very quick but an experience I'll never forget. Of course, I made a nice donation for his special causes. I'm glad I did it, glad I went.

I always tried to attend mass when I was on the road with the A's. At home, I was going to 6:30 AM mass every day at St. Simon's, my parish—at least before the pandemic. And I didn't go alone in recent years; I took my tiny nine-pound Norwich Terrier, Sadie, my best buddy. It was too cold to leave her in the car one morning, so I smuggled her inside in a little carrying case and placed her under the pew. No one knew. I never asked the pastor if animals were allowed, and I prayed to God she didn't make any noise. She was as quiet as a church mouse even when I went up for Communion. I kept bringing her to mass for several years. Sure enough, as soon as I got back to the car, she started yelping.

I'm always thrilled to talk about a distant relative of mine, Father Alfred Boeddeker, who founded St. Anthony's Dining Room in San Francisco's Tenderloin district, which has fed millions since he opened the doors in 1950. He was a great, great human being and priest. I have an article about him in my office, and the headline says it all: GENTLE FRIEND TO NEEDY. Father Boeddeker was my mother's second cousin and my grandmother's first cousin and was pastor at St. Boniface Church in the Tenderloin, an area in San Francisco with high levels of crime, drugs, and homelessness. He tried his best to help the needy and feed the hungry.

St. Anthony's started a farm in Sonoma to supply food for the dining room, and we visited on one of Father Boeddeker's anniversaries in the priesthood. That's where I learned more about his dedication to helping others. St. Anthony's mostly relies on donations, and when I started making a little money, the first million dollars I gave away was to St. Anthony's Dining Room in San Francisco. I wanted to do something in Father Al's honor. I felt it was right. I knew I was helping a wonderful man who was helping others.

Chapter 2

My Family

MY FATHER, EDGAR, STUDIED ENGINEERING at Santa Clara University, and that's why my parents settled in Santa Clara after coming from Petaluma, a town a couple of hours north, where they met.

My parents had three children, and I was the youngest by far. My brother, Larry, was seven and a half years older, and my sister, Dianne, was 18 months older than Larry, nine years older than I. When she was finishing up college, I was just graduating from grammar school. But they were always there for me.

Growing up, Dianne was a recreation director at a park and asked me to come over and help her with different functions. She attended San Jose State, just like my wife, and became an elementary school teacher at Sacred Heart in San Jose.

Santa Clara University was all male then. Like my father, Larry got an engineering degree at Santa Clara, so my brother, father, and brother-in-law, Gene Ravizza, all graduated in engineering. I knew I wasn't smart enough to be an engineer, and we had enough engineers in the family, so we needed someone with business acumen. I studied business.

My father was one of the founders of the city of Santa Clara, and its first registered city engineer, from the 1940s to the 1960s. I was very proud of him. He was widely respected for what he did and the kind of person he was. If I got in trouble, they'd ask my name. I said, "Schott." They said, "Are you the son of the city engineer?" I said, "Yes, that's my father." They said, "Have a nice day." That wouldn't work these days. But back then, Santa Clara was a small town. Everybody knew everybody.

My father's job wasn't a very high-paying position. Public servants got paid very little compared with what they get today. It was a sign of the times. Consequently, our family didn't have a lot of money. When I was born, my father was probably making 300 bucks a month, and he wasn't making more than a thousand a month when I was in college. It was tough, but he loved his job.

"In 1929, the city of Santa Clara had about 4,000 people, a university, and a few industries that were mostly food-processing types that caused heavy sewage flows. The state highway passed through, and there were only three or four paved streets. A new city council, elected on an improvement platform, engaged the dean of the College of Engineering as the city engineer on a commissioner and retention fee to program the work. The dean, George L. Sullivan, engaged me to do the work. I did designs and surveys, and we completed a storm drainage system, sewage system, and treatment plant in 18 months. I was able to take an instructor position at the College of Engineering and continue working for the dean on the city's problems and private engineering work."

—Edgar Schott

My parents had a tough time making ends meet. My brother worked all summer long to make tuition. When I got to college, I had the baseball scholarship, so when I worked in the summertime, I gave my checks to my mom to help with the household expenses. Then I'd ask her for a few bucks if I needed it, if we decided to go out for a pitcher of beer or something.

My wife's father was Joe Sunseri, who had a hand in a lot of significant ventures. He was part owner of the San Jose Speedway, a NASCAR racetrack, and ran a food and beverage concession business that served several venues: Santa Clara County Fairgrounds, San Jose Civic Auditorium, Frontier Village, San Jose Municipal Stadium, and some golf courses. Plus, he helped form the San Jose Bees in the early 1960s, a minor league team that developed a colorful history. He had a lot of connections in the sports world and got tickets to the 1962 Giants-Yankees World Series at Candlestick Park, but I was working my first job, at Ford Motor Company, and was too honest. I should have called in sick. My wife was able to go, though!

I laugh when I hear that Pat and I inherited money from her parents, that "he got his father-in-law's food business." That wasn't the case at all, not one dollar. They needed their money. Joe lived to be 95, Pat's mother 101. Like I said, we had $500 between us when we got married, and I didn't have a checking account until after the wedding. Why would I need one?

When I was a senior in college, I couldn't date Pat because she was working for her father at the speedway on Friday and Saturday nights. I could never go out with her, so I got a job at the speedway because it was the only way I could see her. Plus, it was a way to make a buck rather than sitting around waiting for her to get off work.

We got married in September 1962, 60 years ago, and our three kids—Steve, Lisa Treadwell, and Kristen Kordelos—all had children. Steve's kids are Ryan, Nick, Matt, and Natalie; Lisa's are Trever, Kenny, and Robby; and Kristen's are Michael and Brinley. Plus, we have 10 nieces and nephews, my brother with seven kids and my sister with three. We'd get together for all the major holidays with the different families, and as you can imagine, the gatherings were large and festive.

"Pat couldn't have been nicer during the time Steve owned the A's, couldn't have been more of a sweetheart. She was fantastic. She really enjoyed the game, a real fan. Steve Jr. was really nice too. He was busy working with his dad. He was close to my age and was very respectful to all of us. But it was Pat who really followed the game like crazy. I think she watched more games than me and Steve."

—Billy Beane

Madge Hepburn is like family too. Madge has been with us for 31 years as a housekeeper and caretaker. She has a wonderful story. She came over from Jamaica with three children and didn't know what she was going to do. We needed someone to help us when we moved into our house. Somehow we got word of her, interviewed her, and hired her. Her kids were in elementary school at the time, and she worked hard to become a citizen. All her children went to college, earned master's degrees, and are very successful. Her son, Kevin, got his master's in sports management at San Jose State and started working for us at the A's, and worked himself up to a pretty good position; then the Warriors found out about him and hired him away.

Chapter 3

A Model Child,
My Brother, Larry

I COULDN'T HAVE HAD A BETTER BROTHER. Larry was a super person. You couldn't find a nicer guy. The most solid guy in the world. He got straight A's all the time. I couldn't emulate him; that would have been too hard to achieve. Larry was a tremendous person—the brains, the grades, just a model child. I'd procrastinate, put things off, and it affected my schoolwork. Larry was an exemplary brother. He did a lot for my parents. He was a hard act for me to follow.

Though Larry was seven years older, we used to spend a lot of time together. He was one of my biggest supporters and came to a lot of my ballgames when I was pitching. He's the one who gave me the idea of going into the development and homebuilding business. He went on to have a great family with seven wonderful children and many grandkids.

At the age of 72, in 2005, Larry was stricken by an awful disease and died. It happened so fast, out of the blue. He suddenly had issues with his muscles and memory. His brain was being taken over by the disease. He lost a lot of his physical functions and talked about things that made no sense. He was reverting to his childhood. No doctors around could diagnose what he had, so we brought him to the UCSF Medical Center, and the diagnosis was determined pretty quickly. It was Creutzfeldt-Jakob disease or CJD, an extremely rare neurological disorder—so rare that it affects one person in a million. We didn't know anything about the disease. Not until 30 days before his death did we learn about it, and we learned there was no cure. It was so unfortunate and sad; the disease took Larry away from his great family.

> *"Larry and I were contemporaries. We were the same age and graduated from Santa Clara together in 1953. I knew the family very well. Steve's sister, Dianne, was a good friend of my sister. Larry was a very nice guy, very smart guy. Steve was the good athlete among us. He was just a youngster and would tag along. Larry went into land planning and engineering, kind of tied into what Steve was doing later, and clearly was an inspiration for Steve, who really looked up to him and respected him."*
>
> —Ed Panelli, former California Supreme Court justice

There's another story here. As a young kid, I didn't always do the right things. In some ways, I was a wise-ass kid. There was a knot hole in the fence between our house and the neighbor's, and when I saw the kid next door looking through the hole, I threw a rock his way. The rock went right through the hole and hit the kid. I remember seeing blood. I knew I was in the doghouse. I couldn't have been more than six or seven. If you had given me a thousand rocks, I wouldn't have been able to throw another through that knothole. Sure enough, Larry said we needed to talk to my mom, who spoke with the kid's mother. I had to apologize. It was a big deal. My mom said she was going to send me away to a camp for delinquents. It scared the hell out of me. I don't think I ever tried that again.

Long Schott

Well, the kid I hit was Stephen DeArmond, who became a prominent doctor. A couple of years after Larry died, I ran into Stephen at a Bellarmine reunion. We not only went to high school together but also to St. Clare's grammar school and Santa Clara University, though I really didn't see him in college because he was a medical student, and we took different courses. The reunion was really the first time we crossed paths since we were kids, and we talked about that moment I threw the rock.

> *"I remember watching the rock's curved flight and realized that it was going to go through the knothole and hit me. I moved my head as fast as I could, but the rock hit me under my right eye. I ran to my mother, who marched me to the Schott home to show Mrs. Schott what had happened. Steve had to apologize and buy me a big lollipop. That's what I remembered. Steve said that when he saw the rock go through the small knothole, he became convinced that he was going to be a great baseball player, maybe even a pro. Of course, he could not foresee that he would own a major league team."*
>
> —Stephen DeArmond

Well, I had been wanting to give money to UCSF for research to help find a cure for the disease that took Larry, and somebody referred me to Dr. Stanley Prusiner at the hospital's Institute for Neurodegenerative Diseases. Prusiner, who had been awarded the Nobel Prize in Medicine, said the doctor assigned to that particular cause of CJD was Stephen DeArmond. I said, "What? I know Stephen." He turned out to be the doctor who worked on getting a cure for my brother's disease. It was such an amazing coincidence all the way around. I was going to give $100,000 a year over 10 years, $1 million in all, and it was Stephen who wound up using it for his research. I got to know him a lot better. We talked a couple of times a year, and he is a terrific guy, incredibly smart. They thought they were making progress. Like anything else, it's two steps forward and one step back or one forward and two back. As it turned out, after the ninth year, he was furloughed and never got to finish the 10th year.

> *"My greatest regret is that I was not able to complete the 10th year of the Schott grant. I felt that I had disappointed Steve and Pat Schott by not finding a clue to a treatment for prion diseases."*
>
> —Stephen DeArmond

It was unfortunate they nudged Stephen out of the position. I funded $900,000 of the $1 million grant. They gave up on him being able to come up with a cure, but it's like trying to find a cure for cancer, though this is far rarer. Stephen did great work, and I'll never forget what he did to fight this terrible disease that took my brother.

Chapter 4

I Wanted to Be a Farmer

WHEN I WAS A YOUNGSTER, I thought I'd be a farmer. It was in my blood. I loved the outdoors. Loved the open land. All kids have dreams, and I wanted to farm. We lived on a four-acre prune orchard in Santa Clara, and my parents were from Petaluma, once known as the Chicken Capital of the World. My mother's parents ran a chicken ranch on the west side of Bodega Highway and sold eggs, and we would visit quite often, every three months or so, from the time I was 6 or 7 until I was 12 or 13. That's when farming was my dream.

It was a 10-acre ranch, unbelievably magnificent with incredibly fertile soil, all natural with no additives necessary. My grandparents grew corn and tomatoes, and the soil was unlike the black adobe we had back home, which was hardly fertile. My mother's sister lived about a mile from my grandparents' ranch on King Road, and I often would meet up with that side of the family and run around with my cousins: Eleanor, who was close to my age, and Connie, and Margaret, who were both close in age to my sister, Dianne.

My dad's father was a butcher in Petaluma and died young, when my father was 12. My grandmother had to raise three kids and ran a boarding house to make ends meet. Two of the kids—my father, Edgar, and his sister, Lucille—married two other siblings. It's a bit confusing, but my mom, whose maiden name was Hartman, and her brother, Frank Hartman, married Schotts. That brings me to my cousin, Bob Hartman, whom I actually call my double cousin. His parents, Uncle Frank and Aunt Lucille, got divorced, and Bob was getting in trouble during high school because he wasn't receiving supervision. So my mother took him in, and he lived with us for about a year. I was just a kid but looked up to him and bugged him, I guess because I was impressed with his size—he was 6'5"—and that he played football. He was patient with me.

Bob didn't have good grades, but my mom helped him get into Bellarmine his senior year. The school knew my brother, Larry, and took my mother's word that Bob would be all right. She talked with the football coach, Bill Prentice, and he gave him a little extra look and got him on the team, which might not have happened otherwise. As it turned out, Bob made first string, won a scholarship to Oregon State, and got drafted by the Detroit Lions in 1954. He always remembered what my mother did for him and would come back to visit her.

Another interesting story involves cousins on my father's side. His youngest sister, Alice, married a fellow named Tom Regan, and they had four kids. Uncle Tom, a great guy, brought his family to Lake Tahoe, where he was a manager at Bank of America, funding many businesses, and had a beach named after him on South Shore. After Pat and I got married, we'd journey to Tahoe and contact my Uncle Tom, who brought us to some shows on the strip. Anyway, when he died and my aunt died a few years later, we lost track of the family. Well, we caught up because my sister connected with my cousin, Jean Regan, who lives in San Jose. Her son, Chad, went to Bellarmine and Santa Clara, where I went to school, and she saw the name "Schott" around campus and connected with us to ask if it was the same Schott.

Long Schott

"The good news was his sister had been working on a family tree. Dianne and I became close and shared stories and family photos. We missed a lot of time, a lot of stories, but it was nice reconnecting after all these years. The previous memory I had of all of us being together was in 1967, when my dad was at Stanford Hospital, and we stayed at the Schotts'. We were just kids playing in their family orchard."

—Jean Regan Bourne

Make no mistake. I enjoyed hanging around the Petaluma ranch a lot more than picking prunes in our orchard. I spent a lot of time picking prunes, and it was necessary because we sold them for income. It was common in the valley. My brother and sister were much older, so I often was alone going up and down the rows in the heat of summer when the prunes were ripe. This was long before mechanical harvesters. I was on my hands and knees picking prunes off the ground, putting them into buckets, and transferring them into boxes.

"Picking prunes was a tough job. We knelt for 12 hours a day, 6:00 AM to 6:00 PM, and it wasn't like picking pears off trees. With prunes, they'd shake the branches so the prunes would fall to the ground, and you'd show up with your pail and pick them up. I guess we were too dumb to know we could wear kneepads. You're kneeling on dirt clods with the sun beating on your back while fighting off bees that were attracted to the juice and buzzing around you. But we all did it back then."

—Tom Hastings, lifetime friend

I loved Petaluma, and I've always thought about owning a vineyard. A 570-acre piece of property, once a cattle ranch, across the Bodega Highway from my grandparents' chicken ranch came up for sale when I owned the A's. I had known from my days as a youngster that this was some of the best soil you'd ever come across. I flew my helicopter to the property with Nick Rossi, then chief legal counsel for the A's, who had put me in touch with people up there. Flying over the property, it was gorgeous. I almost bought it but decided against it because I would have wanted a tasting room, and that was impossible because it was at a blind curve in the road with no potential for a driveway for people to enter and taste the wine. It would have been bad access. I never took that step.

In retrospect, it's a regret. I wasn't thinking clearly because I was so heavily involved with the A's and my business. I was thinking about a winery, but I should have been thinking just about a vineyard and adding a winery later, one step at a time. I really should have bought it. It was a mistake. I don't know if it makes sense, but I still look for a vineyard now and then. It's still in my blood.

Chapter 5

The Musical Side
of the Family

I HAVE ANOTHER COUSIN, Bob Regan, who's Jean Regan's older brother and a well-known country songwriter, a big shot in the Nashville country music industry who has written songs for Roy Rogers, Reba McEntire, Tanya Tucker, Billy Ray Cyrus, Keith Urban, George Strait, Luke Bryan, and many others. Bob cowrote "Thinkin' About You," which Trisha Yearwood performed and which climbed to No. 1 on the country chart.

Bob founded a program benefiting veterans, many of whom come home and are struggling with PTSD or don't have opportunities. It's called Operation Song, and it brings songwriters together to help veterans and active military share their stories through song. Bob performed at military bases around the world with the Armed Forces Entertainment tours and has been inspired to do what he can. When I heard about this venture, I wanted to contribute and am proud to say I have helped support the program over the years, another reason it was so wonderful to reconnect with our cousins.

As it turns out, my grandson Nick, a music major at Santa Clara, is trying to make it in the music industry, and he went back to Nashville, where Bob tutored him. My mother loved music and going to musicals and always sang in the house, and my brother played piano and violin and would perform while others gathered around for sing-alongs, so it's great that it has been passed down through the generations.

"I've been blessed to have written some hit songs and, late in my career, have the opportunity to work with veterans through Operation Song. The idea came during my tours of military bases in the mid-2000s. I'd heard some amazing stories and thought, 'Let's put songwriters together with veterans and see what happens.' As a writer, I know that spilling thoughts on paper can help make them make sense and give them order. When you put those thoughts into lyrics, make them rhyme, and put them to music, it can be powerful and often cathartic. The songs can be about something that happened in battle, honoring a fallen brother or sister lost in service, or any story they'd like to tell. It's been an honor to discover something like this, a completely different use of my skill set, and I'm honored Stephen and Patricia are listed among our generous donors. And I'm deeply grateful about the family connections."

—Bob Regan

For me, music was never a serious consideration, though I've loved country music since I was a kid. I can listen to it every night—Merle Haggard, Johnny Cash, the old guys. I used to drink a little beer in college and visited these little taverns, and the guys older than us would be playing country music on the jukebox, and I loved it. Give me rock and roll from the 1950s and '60s too. I wasn't too musically inclined and never took to an instrument. I took piano lessons for three or four years but didn't like the practicing. I wanted to go outside and play ball.

On the other hand, I had a pretty good voice and used to sing in the choir at the local Catholic church. Sometimes I was a little nervous and afraid I'd start in the wrong key and mess up the whole song, but they usually gave you the key to start, the right note, and once I was in key, I was OK. When I was a senior in high school, I had a Jesuit professor who liked the theater, and he got us together one night for a variety show. We performed a song from *H.M.S. Pinafore*, the Gilbert and Sullivan comedy opera that takes place aboard the Royal Navy ship H.M.S. *Pinafore*. We performed "I Am the Captain of the Pinafore," and I played the captain, so I had to do some singing. It was just a little 10-minute skit in the variety show but was well accepted by the local audience. That was the extent of my music career.

Chapter 6

Pass It Down

IF YOU'RE RUNNING A LONGTIME SUCCESSFUL business, it's only natural that you'd like to keep it in the family. I was hoping the lineage would keep going forward for the sake of keeping the business going. I didn't want to turn the business over to a stranger. You feel better when it's family, much better. My son, Steve—we don't say "Junior"; Steve's middle name is Edgar (after my father), and mine is Charles—got his business degree at Santa Clara and then came to work with the companies.

Steve knows more about home construction than I do. He worked summer jobs as a carpenter, and I told him not to tell anyone his last name so there would be no favoritism, no soft jobs. I wanted him to do the same jobs as everyone else, so he was up on roofs in the heat of summer putting up rafters for shake-style roofs and everything else that goes with it. I told Steve if he wanted to join the company, he'd have to start out in the field. Early on, I asked him, "Do you enjoy it here? I don't want you working here if you don't feel it's the right environment." I knew the financial end would be good for him. That was already in place, but he had to make the company grow. He said he did enjoy it. Eventually I said, "OK, you're the quarterback now. Here's the team."

Working together, father and son, can be difficult. We think very differently. I came from a different background, jumping around from company to company and learning all the different facets of the business, starting early when I got a real estate license and sold on weekends. Steve didn't get that same chance. Nobody really does what I did anymore because all those opportunities at different companies no longer are available, but I was never a carpenter like Steve.

Our daughters, Lisa and Kristen, took care of merchandising and marketing of model homes, working with decorators, which we needed. After they got married, they still helped out once in a while, but Steve has been on the entire end of it. Most of the grandkids sought other job opportunities, but Steve's son, Matt, was interested in the field and came to work with us in land acquisition development. So it's now three generations. There's no guarantee it'll last, but it's nice to know the business is in family hands.

"I knew I wanted to go into finance and become an analyst. During summers in college, I worked as a carpenter and learned a lot about the construction trade. I became a framer, putting two-by-fours together and pounding nails into the plates. It was a lot of work. My hands and arms were sore every day. I tell you one thing: those guys worked their butts off. It was a great way to learn the business from the ground up.

"I got my degree in finance at Santa Clara, was doing a little work with my dad's company, and started interviewing for jobs. My dad knew I was interviewing and asked if I liked what I was doing at his company, and I said absolutely. So he said, 'Why don't you come work for me full time?' I said, 'I'd like that.' It's been 34 years. He's been my business mentor. We don't always see eye to eye on things. We have our bouts and make up. I've

got to hand it to my dad. He could have retired long ago but continues to come in the office and work because he loves it. I learned from him that you've got to love what you do or you won't be successful at it. I told my boys that. Pursue careers that you'd enjoy. It's one of the reasons my son Ryan is a fireman. Helping people is his passion. It's the message my dad taught me, and that applies to my other sons—Nick, a musician, and Matt, who now works for me."

—**Steve Edgar Schott**

Speaking of lineage, sports are big throughout the family. In fact, when I owned the A's, I think my family got more fun out of it than I did. They loved the team, loved the players. I was more standoffish because I didn't feel comfortable getting too close to the players. They were the ones performing. But my son, two daughters, and grandkids loved it. It was a great time to be A's fans. The team was a fun-loving group, and our grandkids got opportunities to be batboys in spring training.

Steve played football and basketball in high school and rugby in college, and the grandkids played all kinds of sports. A couple of them— Lisa's son, Kenny, and Kristen's son, Michael—went on to play college baseball. Kenny was a pitcher at Santa Clara, and Michael is a study in perseverance, because he got cut from Santa Clara and transferred to Mission College, where he turned his game around with a 37-game hit streak and conference batting title and was named All–Northern California. He got recruited back to Division I at San Jose State, played a year, and then redshirted and transferred back to Santa Clara.

It's really a fabulous story. Michael opened the 2020 Santa Clara season and was in the lineup 13 of the first 17 games before the pandemic shut everything down. That team went 12–5 and beat Stanford and Georgia, two of the nation's top teams. Then in 2021 it got even better. He homered in each of the season's first three games at UC Santa Barbara, which was ranked nationally. He finished the series with six hits and seven RBIs and was named West Coast Conference Player of the Week. In a game at Santa Clara, he hit a walk-off homer to beat USF, a rival. That USF game, fans couldn't sit in the seats behind the plate because of the pandemic, so Pat went out and watched from beyond the outfield. Michael hit two homers that day, and she wound up with both of the baseballs. I'm impressed by Michael's persistence. It was a long time coming, but he showed if you work hard, good things can happen. If he pursues anything like he pursued baseball, he'll be very successful.

My sister Dianne's grandson Matt Long also played at Santa Clara. My brother Larry's grandson Joey Schott is a pitcher at Baylor.

"I remember being a batboy for Opening Day at the Santa Clara stadium. I grew up around the area, attended Bronco games and watched my two cousins—Matt Long, who made it to Triple A with the Angels and Brewers, and Kenny Treadwell, a hard-throwing pitcher—and looked up to both of them.

"I grew up wanting to be a Bronco. When I got to play there, I didn't want people to know my grandfather's name was on the stadium so there wouldn't be any favoritism. I tried to keep that low-key. Having a different last name helped. One of our hitting coaches came up at the end of 2020 and said, 'I had no idea your grandfather was Steve Schott.' I just wanted to be a good teammate, but I'm so grateful for my grandparents' support. I know they truly care about what the university and community stand for and the Jesuit values. That day I hit the homer to beat USF, I was playing right field and peeked over and saw my grandmother. It's funny. It seems almost every time she was at the game, I would hit a home run. I was glad that after all I went through—as a junior in high school, I got cut from the varsity—I was able to get a full season starting in Division I."

—Michael Bowes, grandson

The Santa Clara University connection, obviously, is prevalent. Many family members have gone to the school, and it started with my father, who was both a student and teacher at Santa Clara. Larry and I went there, as did my sister's husband and all seven of Larry's kids. So did two of my kids (my youngest, Kristen, went to USD), as did three of Steve's kids and other grandkids went there too, including those who played baseball. Nobody pushed them to go. Maybe some didn't feel like going far away to school. It's a great place to go and provides a great education while creating the opportunity to make lifelong friends.

For example, when the Giants came to San Francisco in 1958, I remember attending a game with my brother and his friend and seeing a left-handed pitcher who was fooling a lot of hitters. I really liked the way he pitched. His name was Mike McCormick, and he went on to win a Cy Young Award in 1967. It turned out McCormick's son, Matt, and my son, Steve, became very good friends, both going to St. Francis High School and Santa Clara, where they were roommates. I ran into McCormick a couple of times when he was at the baseball field to watch Matt pitch. People referred to Matt as Mike McCormick's son, and Steve always teased him about it and nicknamed him Son Of. Like, "Hey, Son Of, what are you doing?" So when I bought the A's, Steve was written up in the paper for his role in running the residential development department for the business, and he was referred to as "the son of A's owner Steve Schott." Well, Matt McCormick started calling Steve Son Of. It was pretty good payback.

Chapter 7

A Sports Fan through the Years

WHEN I LISTENED TO SAN FRANCISCO SEALS games as a kid, my favorite player was a guy named Les Fleming, who had spent 10 years in the majors with the Tigers, Indians, and Pirates. I was 10, 11 years old, and these guys were my heroes much more than major leaguers because the major leagues were so far away. This was 1950, eight years before the Giants and Dodgers came west, and Fleming was the Seals' first baseman. We didn't get a TV until later in the '50s, so our connection with these guys was through radio broadcasts. I don't know why I liked Les Fleming so much. Maybe because he hit a lot of home runs and sounded so legendary over the radio.

As a birthday present, my mom and brother brought me to Seals Stadium, my first professional game, so I was going to get a chance to see Les Fleming, who was in his mid-30s. It's funny because he didn't look like the guy I anticipated. I anticipated a tall, strapping guy. He was short and dumpy. I guess I was a little disappointed, because he was a Seal who actually had the shape of a seal. My mother and brother were kidding me that my hero was the mascot.

I started taking a liking to Bob Thurman. He was an outfielder who played in the Negro Leagues for the legendary Homestead Grays and made his major league debut with the Cincinnati Reds in his late 30s. In between, he played a couple of years with the Seals, and he was fun to watch. Leo Righetti, the father of the pitcher and longtime pitching coach Dave Righetti, was an excellent shortstop for the Seals for a few years. Leo went to my old high school, Bellarmine, and I got to know Dave a little from the Los Altos Country Club, a really nice guy. Those Coast League games were so exciting. Seals Stadium was in the Mission District at 16th and Bryant, a beautiful little ballpark, and an awesome place to watch baseball.

The rivalry between the Seals and Oakland Oaks was a big thing. Sometimes they'd play split doubleheaders on the weekend—one game in the morning, and then they'd hop on the ferry to cross the bay and play another game in the afternoon. I didn't like the Oaks. I was a Seals fan. You picked sides.

The Seals were around from 1903 until 1957 and then had to move to Phoenix because the Giants were coming in 1958. It took a couple of years to build Candlestick Park, so the Giants played at Seals Stadium in 1958 and 1959. By then I was in college, and it was a great place to take a date. Two or three of us asked some nurses who were part-time students at Santa Clara if they were baseball fans, and we all wound up at Seals Stadium. I guess I liked it so much because it was so cozy. It was one level and very intimate, a neighborhood park, and obviously very suited for the Giants when they arrived.

Then they moved to Candlestick, and that wasn't so cozy. We remained Giants fans—the A's didn't arrive until 1968—and I loved to watch Juan Marichal pitch with his high leg kick and big assortment of deceiving pitches. Orlando Cepeda and Willie McCovey were coming up, and Willie Mays was the established star, of course. They were such an exciting team, and they started coming over to Santa Clara to play exhibitions every year. It was orchestrated by the college president, Father Patrick A. Donohoe, and the Giants' owner, Horace Stoneham, who was a member of the university's board of regents, and they played on campus at Buck Shaw Stadium for much of the 1960s and '70s. The Giants' third baseman in the early '70s, Al Gallagher, came out of Santa Clara University.

It was a big deal every time the Giants showed up. Crowds were as big as 11,000, and the Broncos managed to win a few. Here's a story Santa Clara alumni like to tell: In one of the exhibitions, Pete Magrini struck out Willie Mays and later pitched a few games for the Red Sox, and Nelson Briles pitched very well over five innings, got signed by the Cardinals, and enjoyed a long career in the majors. He won 19 games in 1968 and pitched in the World Series along with Ray Washburn, my summer ball teammate in Alberta, Canada, during my college days.

"Yeah, I remember playing at Santa Clara. Mr. Stoneham knew the priests over there, so we'd play the kids in exhibition games. I enjoyed playing with those guys. I remember a kid struck me out. Good fastball, man. There were some laughs. If I remember correctly, I might've come up next time, and the guy threw me the same pitch, and I hit it over a little warehouse in the outfield. I didn't run around the bases. I ran to first base and kept running straight to the clubhouse. I was tired, man. We didn't want to use a lot of energy because we were trying to stay strong for the season."

—Willie Mays, Hall of Famer

I continued going to Giants games over the years and continued to freeze at Candlestick. I got seats down behind the plate, then I made a little more money and got a suite for the season that I later converted to a football box for 49ers games. It was tough to pull off. This is when

Bob Lurie owned the Giants, and his wife, Connie, helped hook me up. I got to know them through the Vintage Club in Indian Wells. It was a unique setup. We were behind home plate for baseball and in the corner of the end zone for football, and it was nice because I didn't have to relocate or move my personal belongings out.

It was a great time because these were the Joe Montana and Steve Young years. It was phenomenal. I had followed 49ers quarterbacks Y.A. Tittle in the 1950s and John Brodie in the '60s and '70s, but Joe got them to the next level and won all those Super Bowls. And then Steve won one. It was a little easier to get Super Bowl tickets back then, and we got to quite a few. We went to a lot of Raiders games in the 1970s, but the 49ers were the team of the '80s.

San Francisco baseball was thriving then too, and the Giants got to the playoffs a couple of times in the late '80s and played the A's in the 1989 World Series. I stopped being a Giants fan in 1995, the year I bought the A's. I still admired a lot of people on the Giants, and that includes Dusty Baker, their manager during most of my time with the A's. I remember we ran into each other at a private terminal after Game 2 of the 2002 World Series in Anaheim, and I told him, "I sure hope you win the World Series—not for the Giants' sake but for your sake." He thanked me. I really liked him. Dusty's such a gentleman, a pleasant guy. They didn't win the Series, but they won their share later under Bruce Bochy.

Part Two

PLAYING BALL

Chapter 8

"Can You Pitch?"

WHEN I WAS A KID, I didn't dream of owning a baseball team. My dream was working my way up to the major leagues as a player.

My brother would play softball in the street with a lot of buddies. I'd always be out there trying to get in a game. They were very patient with me. That's where I started playing the sport. I didn't play organized ball until I was a freshman in high school, at an all-boys seminary in Mountain View, St. Joseph's. It's where Tom Brady's father, Tom Sr., went to school, a few years after I did. It was a boarding school, and visitors were allowed just once a month, a tough disciplinary for the priesthood. When you're that young, you don't know what you want to do, and I had been encouraged by my local pastor to go to the seminary.

So they asked me, "Can you pitch?" I told them I had never pitched competitively but I could try. For some reason, I had a natural sinker. If I kept the ball low, it would sink. I didn't know why. People said I had a heavy ball. I didn't know what that meant. I didn't have any formal coaching or real guidance on pitching of any kind. That's what it was like in those days. They just gave me the ball and told me to pitch.

The technology available today would have really helped; it would have made a world of difference if I had information on how to pitch a guy. I've learned so much about pitching just watching these guys on television. We never had film like this. It's amazing. We just took the mound blind, without a clue, and went with our best stuff. I watched other guys pitch to learn how and learned to keep hitters off-balance. I really enjoyed it and had some success. I developed a big roundhouse curveball, and some of the guys had never seen that before. I'd aim at the right-handed hitter, and it would break to the outside corner. But left-handers saw it coming and weren't fooled much.

After my freshman year, I played Pony League in the summer. They gave us a cap and T-shirt, and that was it. You were out there playing in your Levi's. We had to go find enough guys to form a team in Santa Clara, and we'd play against other teams from San Jose.

I got to be good enough that the legendary coach from Bellarmine College Prep, Bob Fatjo, saw me pitch and asked about coming to Bellarmine, a Catholic high school in San Jose that has had some great baseball teams. More than a dozen kids from Bellarmine have gone on to play in the majors, including three guys I was familiar with—Marv Owen, Wayne Belardi, and Jim Small, all of whom wound up with the Detroit Tigers. Belardi broke in with the Brooklyn Dodgers but didn't play much because he was a first baseman and backed up Gil Hodges.

More recently, Pat Burrell, Eric Thames, Kevin Frandsen, and Mark Canha have come out of Bellarmine. It was an independent school when I was there, so we didn't play league games and didn't have playoffs, but we always had good records. A couple of schools in San Francisco were comparable: St. Ignatius and Sacred Heart.

So Fatjo came up to me after a Pony League game and asked if I was going back to the seminary or if I'd go to Bellarmine. My brother graduated from Bellarmine, so I had interest. I was pretty tall and skinny, 6'0" and probably 160 pounds. Fatjo said I wouldn't make the varsity—he didn't see me playing against competitive varsity players yet—but said if I was good enough on JV, there was a good chance he'd bring me up during the year. And that's exactly what happened. My JV coach was Bill McPherson, a good guy who had played football at Santa Clara and later became a very respected coach under Bill Walsh with the San Francisco 49ers and was part of five Super Bowl championships.

Jim Small was a great player at Bellarmine, very fast and a good defender in the outfield with good pop in his bat. Marv Owen, the first from Bellarmine to make the majors, later became a Tigers scout and signed Jim, who went right from high school to Detroit.

> *"We had a lot of good players. We played freshman teams at Stanford, Cal, and San Jose State and the public high schools. I remember Steve as a damn good pitcher, one of the top two during my years, along with Jim Gill. You knew Steve was gonna be good. He had a lot of moxie. Good sinking fastball, good competitor. He was smarter than hell. I knew guys on the honor roll; I was always leery of them. A damn good student. I wasn't. Good students hung together. Steve was pretty straight. I was too, to a certain degree."*
>
> —Jim Small, outfielder for the
> 1955–57 Detroit Tigers and 1958 Kansas City A's

I thought we were going to have a great pitching staff my junior year. Jim Gill, Frank Cornell, Dick Polhemus. I was the fourth starter, but things happened to everyone else, including Gill breaking his collarbone in football, and I suddenly wound up as the No. 1 pitcher (9–3 record, 1.67 ERA, named to All-City first-team). It was Small's senior year, and we went 28–7.

We lost a lot of talent going into my senior year and had no big star in the outfield. The team didn't do that great, but we won more than we lost. I was named Player of the Year and All-City by the *San Jose*

Mercury (8–3 record, 1.05 ERA, five shutouts) and was named to the all-Catholic team by the *Monitor*, a Bay Area Catholic newspaper. My mother was afraid I'd get a big head because the high school teams were written up a lot.

Fatjo had an influence on me both positively and negatively. He was a very good coach, but he didn't win any awards for being complimentary. He was always on your butt; he'd jump on guys. We'd be warming up for a game, and he'd say, "You guys look like a bunch of bush leaguers." I thought that was pretty rough. He wasn't strong dealing with young people, and he would carry you down. He told me one time, "You know, Schott, I'm not sure you can pitch in college," which I didn't think was a good thing to say to a young kid. He didn't build up your self-confidence, which I'm not sure I had much of, but I played for him my junior and senior years of high school and felt good about what I did, including throwing a no-hitter against Salinas High.

Chapter 9

The Story of Curt Flood

AMERICAN LEGION WAS EXTREMELY POPULAR for high school kids when I was growing up, and I vividly recall many of those games and moments. Even the ones I should probably forget, such as the time Curt Flood homered off me.

My team, San Jose Memory Post 399, was playing a team from Stockton. I couldn't find the plate in the first inning and was walking guys. I remember it so well. Sometimes with these old fields, it took a while to get used to the mound. There was a fellow in the stands who played a lot of ball, Len Scarpelli, whose younger brother, Kevin, was on the team. The bases were loaded with nobody out, and Len walked around the dugout and told our coach, "I think I can help this guy." He asked if he could come out and talk with me, and the coach agreed.

So Len came out and said, "I think you're a little bit wild."

I said, "A *little* bit wild?"

So he said, "Steve, try stepping to the right of the mound, because everything you're throwing is outside." I moved over, found the strike zone, struck out the next three guys, and ended up throwing a no-hitter.

One of the great things about American Legion was the opportunity to face players you wouldn't see in your own league. I remember pitching to Curt Flood, the great Gold Glove center fielder who played for the St. Louis Cardinals during the 1960s, a major part of three of their World Series teams.

Curt played for Bill Erwin Post 337 in Oakland, and his coach was George Powles, who coached legendary players over the years—including Frank Robinson, Joe Morgan, and Vada Pinson, as well as Bill Russell. Powles coached both baseball and basketball at McClymonds High School and ran the American Legion team in the summer, and his teams won the American Legion national championships in both 1949 and 1950 in Omaha, Nebraska. J.W. Porter, who played a half dozen years in the big leagues, was the big hitter on those championship teams, and a very young Frank Robinson was on that 1950 team.

Curt played American Legion ball in the mid-'50s and led the Oakland team to a state title in 1955. Well, we played Curt's team at Bushrod Park in Oakland, and they were loaded with talent, so much better than us and far more advanced. I remember one at-bat with Curt in particular. Runners were at second and third, and I quickly fell behind two balls and no strikes. The thing is, I had faced Curt earlier in the game and gotten him out, but I didn't know this was Curt because he had changed his uniform after ripping his pants. My teammates were telling me to walk him, and I was saying no because I was still confident I could get him out. I didn't realize it was Curt. My teammates were right. I threw it pretty fast, and he went the opposite way, hit the fence in right field, and legged out an inside-the-park home run. We lost that game pretty badly.

Let me tell you best part. I ran into Curt years later playing in a pro-am golf tournament in Reno. I was in a foursome with Curt, a best-ball format. Ron Calcagno, who played baseball and football at Santa Clara University and was a successful high school football coach, was also in the foursome. It was funny. Curt didn't play much golf then; he was in his 50s, and he teed it up on the fairway. We told him he probably shouldn't do that. Anyway, we got to talking, and what a really nice guy. He told me a story about his mother. He got a complimentary set of clubs delivered to her house. You play ball, you get gifts like that. His mother opened the clubs and thought they were table ornaments and put them out. She thanked Curt for the gift and put them in a beautiful vase in the living room, and he told her they weren't table ornaments and to take them down and put them in the garage.

That's priceless, isn't it? We laughed. I told Curt his mother must be a wonderful lady. It was an honor to play golf with him. He meant so much to the history of baseball, more for what he did off the field than on. I became a baseball owner but respected the sacrifice he made. He gave up his whole career for all major league players, and he didn't get anything for it, by challenging baseball's reserve clause that prohibited players from signing with other teams when their contracts expired. Teams could pay you whatever they wanted and keep you for as long as they wanted.

Curt contested his trade to the Phillies, and the Supreme Court ruled against him, but he created momentum for the removal of the reserve clause in the mid-1970s and the start of free agency. Good for Curt. I really enjoyed Curt. He was an amazing guy.

Chapter 10

Getting Noticed by the Scouts

WHEN I WAS A SENIOR AT BELLARMINE, toward the end of the season, I hurt my arm. We were playing Richmond, and Bob Fatjo told us all to go out and warm up, to stop lingering and stop talking. I started throwing too hard, too fast. I could feel my shoulder pull and knew something was wrong. I started the game, and it started bothering me after a couple of innings. I kept pitching and shut them out, but I thought, "Oh, God, what did I do?"

It bothered me through the rest of the season. At the time, I had no idea what it was. Looking back, I think I had a slight tear in my rotator cuff, and I didn't even know what that was then.

I usually played American Legion after the school year, but I didn't pitch at all that summer. I didn't want Santa Clara to know my arm was bad. I would not have maintained the scholarship. I was worried I'd hurt it again. It was hard to get it out of my mind, so I let it heal all summer. No throwing at all. Somehow, it healed up. It didn't bother me again until I was a senior in college. Thankfully, there was no problem my first three years.

You couldn't play varsity as a freshman, but it didn't matter, because when I pitched on the freshman team, I was terrible. I couldn't pitch worth a damn. Tremendous control issues, and I was not very effective at all. So I played a lot of outfield. It kept me occupied. I wasn't a great hitter—no big swing, no power to speak of—but got my bat on the ball. But something weird happened after my freshman year.

As soon as summer rolled around, I started playing during the week on a team with ex-pros and junior college guys, and everything changed. I faced a team of ex-pros, older guys who were retired or semiretired, and I was striking them out. The control was impeccable. I got a new lease on life. My buddy Joe Palma and I talked about trying out for the *San Francisco Examiner*'s Northern California All-Star team, which was going to play the San Francisco All-Stars at Big Rec in Golden Gate Park.

My brother and his buddy drove me to the three tryouts—one in Redwood City, one in Vallejo, and one in San Rafael, up in Marin County, where I was dynamite. I struck out five of the six batters I faced, and they told me, "Don't come back. We saw enough of you." I was pretty naive: I didn't take it like I made the team. I grew up on a small ranch; people would give me a razzing, call me a farm boy. I thought I needed to do more to impress them, but they were saying I had made the team.

John Boccabella, who played 12 years in the big leagues, was on that team. So was an outfielder out of Watsonville and Oregon State named Grimm Mason. We ran into each other on the train to the city, and he asked, knowing I was a pitcher, what I was doing with a bat. I said I always brought a bat with me in case I got a chance to hit. Well, he needed a bat, and I told him, "Maybe you'd like this bat." He used it, got some hits, and was one of two players from our team picked to go back to New York and play at another All-Star event. He asked if he could take the bat with him, and I said sure. He later thanked me but said he didn't do as well as he had hoped and broke the bat. He ended up signing with the New York Mets and played a few years in their farm system.

I pitched well in the *Examiner* game, threw hard, and struck out a lot of guys. I came in to pitch after Norm Bass, a big baseball-football star from Vallejo who later pitched for the Kansas City A's. (His brother, Dick Bass, was a running back with the Rams.) I pitched three innings, and when I came out, some scouts came over and asked if I'd be interested in pro ball. They were Charlie Wallgren of the Red Sox, Eddie Bockman and Eddie Montague of the Phillies, and another scout from the Cubs. I was a young guy, barely 18.

I didn't know this, but Bob Fatjo, my high school coach, moonlighted as a birddog scout for the Yankees, and I heard that's why we had pinstripe uniforms at Bellarmine. They came from one of the Yankees farm teams. I'd get little notes in the mail with questionnaires from Tony Robello, the Yankees' main scout in the area, and it was funny because I had wondered where he got all this inside information on me. Well, it was from Fatjo. He was supposed to be one of the coaches on our *Examiner* All-Star team but couldn't come out because of health issues, but he was in touch with Robello. Fatjo asked me, "Why didn't you fill out the questionnaire?" I said, "I didn't think it was that important." I thought I'd take my time. I knew I couldn't sign. I told all the scouts I was staying in school. I had promised my mother that I would get a college degree. But it pumped me up pretty good.

I still wasn't getting help from coaches. People who thought they knew something about pitching, like some of the scouts, gave me a little tweak here and there. Marv Owen with the Tigers, for example. He wasn't a pitcher but said I had a herky-jerky motion, too much arm, and tried to help me. He said that was the worst thing I could do, that's how I could hurt my arm. Well, I already knew about that.

Chapter 11

A College "Change-Over"

WHEN I GOT OLDER, I changed my delivery. I couldn't throw a curveball anymore, and it became more of a slider and got there more quickly with more spin. One of my better pitches at the end was a change-up. If you can deceive the hitter and have a good enough fastball, you can throw them off with your change-up.

My mother never knew much about pitching but thought she did. Lou Lucas was one of my brother's close friends and a catcher at Bellarmine and Santa Clara, and my mom told him, "Now, Lou, help Steve with his change-over." She called it a change-over. The change-over—or change-up—helped me a lot my last two years in college. If I couldn't get my slider over and if my fastball wasn't sinking, I had to have an out pitch, and the change-up came out in such a way you couldn't tell if it was a fastball or not. I still had no pitching coach. It was my best against their best. I just went out there and tried to get by the first couple of innings, get in a groove, and get deep into the game. With that change-up, if I missed on it and got it up high and the timing was off, it was goodbye, baby. So Lou made sure to tell me, "You've got to get that change-over down."

I thought we did a pretty good job building up the program at Santa Clara, which hadn't won a lot in recent years, but it took a little while. Right after I got my scholarship, the coach, Chuck Bedolla, who had been a good athlete at Santa Clara, was fired and replaced by Bill Leonard, a catcher in the Pacific Coast League who thought we should be treated like pros—just go out and play, no discipline or anything. Well, Bill was a good friend of Duane Pillette, who played at Santa Clara before pitching eight years in the big leagues, and he later ran a bar in Los Gatos called the Black Watch. I never had a coach serving us beer, but that was Leonard. I didn't become 21 until I was a senior. I guess he didn't know my age, so we drank beer with the coach at the Black Watch. That's crazy, isn't it? Leonard was let go after my senior year.

It might seem odd now, but we played in two conferences at the same time: the West Coast Athletic Conference and the California Intercollegiate Baseball Association. The CIBA was far more competitive and had five teams, and the other four now are major schools in the Pac-12: Cal, Stanford, USC, and UCLA. USC was the power under legendary coach Rod Dedeaux. Why Santa Clara was in that conference, I never knew. But we hung with them.

My sophomore year, 1958, USC was ranked No. 1 in the country and won the national championship. They had future major leaguers Don Buford and Ron Fairly and a pitcher named Pat Gillick, who got elected to the Hall of Fame as an executive after building World Series championship teams in Toronto and Philadelphia. I remember facing USC as a reliever one game that year. We were way behind when I came in, about five runs, and I shut them down for six or seven innings, allowing us to take the lead. My friend Dick Creighton came in and had two outs in the ninth but gave up a three-run homer, and they beat us, a heartbreaker. That's the way it goes. It would have been nice to say we beat the No. 1 team in the country, but I do remember Dick beating USC our junior and senior years.

> *"I blew it for Steve. USC scored like eight runs the first two innings, and Steve came in and pitched heroically for six-plus innings. We started chipping away, and our first baseman, Mike Birmingham, hit a grand slam. So we're up 11–9, and I come out of the bullpen in the ninth with runners at first and second. A guy pops to left for the second out. John Werhas, who played for the Dodgers and Angels, is on second and takes off for third. Our catcher, Eddie Allen, throws to the bag, where Mike Shea has his glove on this guy's forehead for about three feet. He looks out, game's over. 'Safe,' the ump says. 'Oh, c'mon.' The next guy comes up—Bob Santich, a second-string catcher. Eddie keeps calling fastballs so he can have a chance to throw the guy out at second. I didn't like throwing too many fastballs in a row, and I throw a curve, and it's not a very good one. The guy hits it down the left-field line, and I'm trying to will it foul. But it's a three-run homer, and we lose 12–11. Steve didn't get the win, and Birmingham didn't get the accolades. They were two broken-hearted Broncos, and I had no place to hide."*
>
> —Dick Creighton

My junior year, we had an All-American outfielder, Jim O'Rourke, and an excellent pitching staff, and we went 23–13 and advanced to the NCAA playoffs for the first time in school history. USC was a great team again but deemed ineligible for the NCAAs and supported us as the team to go from our conference. We competed well against them. The two best hitters I faced were on USC: Ron Fairly and Len Gabrielson. The latter was raised in Oakland, played for the Giants and Dodgers, and is now my neighbor. Funny story: I had no idea he was a neighbor until his dog got lost one day and visited my dog, both labs, and my wife got the number on his dog's tag and called Len's wife. Our dogs brought us together, and it was great to connect after all these years; he's a really good guy.

> *"I can literally throw a ball to Steve's house. That's how close we live to each other. We got to know each other better and played several rounds of golf together. We're both lousy. But he has a temperament that always seems controlled. In control of his emotions, at least on the golf course. If he missed a putt, it was, 'All right, I'll try to do better next time.' We had great rivalries in college, and we had a lot of battles with Santa Clara, which was the one Dedeaux wanted to beat all the time. Well, he wanted to beat everybody, and he usually did."*
>
> —Len Gabrielson

We played Fresno State in the first round of the NCAAs and got killed, but I believe we set the groundwork for what was to come with the program.

> *"Our '59 team was better than our '58 championship team. Everybody we played, we beat 'em pretty bad. We thought we were going back to the College World Series, but Coach Dedeaux got a telegram saying USC no longer could go to Omaha because the whole athletic program was on probation by the NCAA because of a violation on the football team—it had something to do with players selling their tickets to alumni and getting big bucks. I was on the football team but not involved with that. No, I wasn't rich in college. But the baseball team suffered because of that. Instead of us, Santa Clara was selected to go to the playoffs. I remember them. I remember the name Steve Schott. We knew the other players because back then, all we did on the bench was yell and scream. We used to be able to get on opposing players, and that's what we did. It was big-time bench jockeying."*
>
> —Don Buford, who played 10 years in the majors and won a World Series with the 1970 Baltimore Orioles

My senior year, Creighton was the No. 1 lefty, and I was the No. 1 righty. Dick had an assortment of pitches. He didn't throw hard but was crafty. He had been in the service and was two years older than I was. Two years means the world at that age, and he was a very smart guy. He knew he wanted to be a teacher and coach. He was much more advanced than I was as a pitcher and went into the Washington Senators system. I always thought Dick could have pitched in the majors. He had a good arsenal of pitches and did very well in pro ball, but because they didn't have a lot of money invested in him, they didn't give him the same chance as others. He could set up guys with a lot of different pitches and, before you knew it, sneak a fastball by you.

> *"We were kind of bookends, a lefty and righty. I was the opposite of Steve, more off speed, a pretty good curveball, kept the ball away from bats. Steve was bigger than I was and threw a heavier ball. The fastball had a lot of movement. I played catch with the guy, and it was like a shot put. That sinker got a lot of groundballs, a lot of broken bats."*
>
> —Dick Creighton

After I graduated, Santa Clara took it to the next level under John "Paddy" Cottrell, a very good coach who came back to the program after coaching at Santa Clara following World War II. During the time in between, he scouted for the Texas Rangers. In 1962, two years after I graduated, Cottrell's team had some great players and won the conference and went to the 1962 College World Series, and I don't think a lot of those players would have gone to the school if not for how well we had done. The World Series team had five guys who went to the major leagues: infielders Ernie Fazio, John Boccabella, and Tim Cullen and pitchers Bob Garibaldi and Pete Magrini, all from the Bay Area.

Fazio, Boccabella, and Garibaldi went right from Santa Clara to the big leagues. Fazio was out of Oakland and played for the Houston Astros' first team, then the Colt .45s. Boccabella was from Marin and played the longest, mostly with the Cubs and Expos, and converted from first base to catcher. Garibaldi came from Stockton and pitched briefly with the Giants. As for the other two guys, Cullen was from Serra High in San Mateo, which later produced Tom Brady and Barry Bonds, and played mostly with the Senators, and Magrini came from Santa Rosa and pitched a few games for the Red Sox.

"At the time, there was a lot of interest in Santa Clara sports, and a lot of us went to the games. Steve was a good pitcher—he's in the school's Athletics Hall of Fame and the San Jose Sports Hall of Fame—and the success of the teams he played on pushed us to prominence in the next era. Jim Sweeters, a Jesuit priest who was the VP of student affairs and acting athletic director, went out and recruited a number of great high school seniors to Santa Clara. Fazio was all set to go to USC. It also helped we played in the CIBA with all those teams now in the Pac-12; it put us on a higher plane. These recruits became the nucleus of Paddy Cottrell's team that finished one out from winning the whole thing."

—Jerry Kerr, class of 1961
and Santa Clara alumni director

That 1962 team not only played in the College World Series but reached the championship game, losing to Michigan 5–4 in 15 innings. Garibaldi was the World Series MVP after throwing nearly nine hitless innings in the title game, only to have the game decided on a ball that was misplayed in the outfield. USC won the national title in both 1961 and 1963, but it was Santa Clara that got to the final game in '62. The CIBA lasted until 1966, and in 1968 Santa Clara began a string of five straight West Coast Athletic Conference titles. Santa Clara's now in the WCC and has more conference titles and NCAA appearances than any team in the conference except Pepperdine.

Speaking of Lou Lucas, who worked on my "change-over," he later volunteered in the university's athletic department for many years with travel arrangements. And his sister, Gerri, had a hand in tipping off Santa Clara University to recruiting its finest athlete ever. She was living in Canada and told Lou that the university should check out this high school kid, and Lou got word to Dick Davey, an assistant basketball coach at the time who became the head coach. I remember my brother, Larry, telling me this story. Well, that kid turned out to be two-time NBA Most Valuable Player and Hall of Famer Steve Nash.

Chapter 12

A Memorable Summer in Canada

RAY WASHBURN OF THE ST. LOUIS CARDINALS pitched a no-hitter at Candlestick Park, and I'll never forget that for a couple of reasons. Number one, he no-hit the Giants a day after Gaylord Perry no-hit the Cardinals. Back-to-back days in 1968, something that had never been done. Number two, Ray Washburn was my teammate on the Lethbridge White Sox in 1959.

After my junior year in college, my buddy Dick Creighton was going to go play for a team in Canada and was told by a guy connected with the team that they needed another pitcher, so he recruited me to play ball for the summer in the Southern Alberta Baseball League. At least we thought it was for the summer. When we got there, we heard a different story. They told us we had to try out for the team. Holy criminy. We hadn't gone all the way up there for a tryout.

We had hopped on a Greyhound bus and took off from San Francisco for the 40-hour drive. It was one heck of a ride. We picked up guys along the way, making stops in Nevada, Montana, and Idaho before pulling into Alberta. We got to the bus station at an odd hour, early in the morning, and were told by the bookkeeper at the bus station to go get a room at the local YMCA and that the guy we were supposed to meet in the morning was Gary Kirk, the manager of the Greyhound bus station and business manager of the Lethbridge White Sox. Well, the YMCA wasn't a nice place. We slept on cots, and rats were running around, so we got the hell out of there after one night.

Later that morning, we came back to meet with Gary Kirk, and he wasn't expecting us. He had no record of Creighton or me and said he had his guys. "Wait a minute. What are we supposed to do? We didn't come here just on a whim. We had bus tickets sent to us. We're not making up this story." We told him how the guy connected with the team set it up with Dick and gave us bus tickets. Gary Kirk told us that guy no longer was affiliated with him and never told him anything about us. Gary said, "I'll tell you what. I'll give your names to the manager of the White Sox. He might want to see you."

I was thinking, "I gave up a union summer job working on a survey crew at my brother's office to come up here for a tryout?" I had worked on the crew the previous summers when I was going to Santa Clara, and I'd pitch at night in local semipro leagues. But this time I had given it up to go to Canada and pitch, but we found out there was no guarantee.

"True story. I hired American kids to come up and play ball—18, 19 years old. We drove them all over and played a lot of games. There was no guarantee we were going to keep Steve. All we did was send Steve Schott and Dick Creighton bus tickets. They had to try out to make the team. Well, they made it, so they stayed."

—Gary Kirk

First game, we traveled a couple of hours to Medicine Hat, and I pitched a 10-inning shutout, and we won 1–0. That clinched my position on the team. I guess if I hadn't lasted the first inning, I'd have been on another bus home. Dick pitched well too, and made the All-Star team. They asked what was supposed to be our financial arrangement, and we said we were supposed to get $350 a month. They said they'd pay us $295, maybe $300, but then they made a compromise and gave us $325. The NCAA never found out about it, thankfully. You weren't supposed to get paid for playing ball while you were in college.

We had a good team—some college players, including a few on the Fresno State team that had just knocked us off in the NCAAs, and local Canadian guys who were pretty good. A lot of those Canadians could swing the bat well because they grew up playing hockey. If they connected with the ball, they'd hit it hard, because hockey had given them strong arms and wrists.

> *"We made the team and had a silent pledge. We knew there would be a lot of pitchers trying to get innings, and we pledged to win 20 games between us, and we did."*
> —Dick Creighton

Our pitching rotation was me, Dick, and Ray Washburn, who went on to play 10 years in the big leagues and pitch in the World Series in 1967, 1968, and 1970. Ray was quite good. When he was on, he was unbeatable. But he had a little arm trouble and had to go back home to the state of Washington. In a game in late July, Washburn threw a no-hitter, nine years before his no-hitter at Candlestick. This one was at Medicine Hat, and he walked eight guys. We won 9–2, and a brawl broke out in the eighth inning. It got pretty ugly, an unfortunate situation.

Sherwood "Woody" Brewer, who played in the Negro Leagues, was the second baseman on the Medicine Hat team and got extremely mad and said racial slurs were coming from our dugout. He went to the plate umpire and our manager, George Wesley, and then Brewer and other players came over to our dugout. At first, I didn't know what he was mad about. Then one of our players, Mountie Bedford, a very good athlete from Fresno State, came out with a bat. It became a big brawl, and fans tried to join in. Brewer and Bedford were ejected, along with the guy Brewer accused of making racist remarks: my buddy Dick Creighton.

I never heard any remarks, and I know Dick didn't make those remarks because I sat next to him all the time when neither of us was pitching. Dick denied it and asked that the accusations be retracted. Medicine Hat tried to get him extradited back to the U.S. Nothing came of it. It was written up in the papers, and the umpires said they didn't hear anything regarding racial slurs from our dugout. It was a shame it all happened. I never knew if there were remarks coming from somewhere else in our dugout. I hope not. I felt for Brewer either way.

"That was a long night. That was a strange game. We were all rooting for Ray to throw a no-hitter, and there was a lot of noise coming out of our dugout because the Medicine Hat pitcher was wild, and we were getting on him. That's what you did. But it was nothing directed at anybody like they were saying. It was, "Ball four, ball four!" The pitcher was pretty frustrated. Brewer was a long way away at second base, thought he heard something, and started mouthing off at our dugout, mentioning my name and Bedford's name. I don't know where it all came from. Medicine Hat said I was getting deported. Our manager was pretty influential and said if they didn't shut up, a lot of people would go to court. We played them two or three more times, and nothing else happened. It settled down."

—Dick Creighton

Long Schott

I mean, Brewer was a well-known and respected player who played for a lot of Negro League teams before we faced him in 1959. The next year, he became manager of the Kansas City Monarchs, the legendary team that once featured Satchel Paige and many other greats. That was Jackie Robinson's team before he signed with the Dodgers. Buck O'Neil played and managed the Monarchs, and Brewer became their final manager in the early '60s.

Our Lethbridge team actually played the Monarchs in an exhibition. They came through, and I had the honor of pitching against them for four innings. I remember doing very well, and we beat them. They were tough competitors, but it obviously was past the heyday of the Negro Leagues, as their fans were turning to the major leagues, which had integrated with Jackie Robinson back in 1947. That experience still meant a lot to me. I was just a kid but had known the Monarchs were one of the legendary teams at the height of the Negro Leagues.

I finished the summer with a good record (10–1) and sometimes felt unhittable, and it was nice that Loyd Christopher, a scout from the Kansas City A's, saw some games I pitched. But all three of us did well (Creighton was 10–3 and Washburn was 9–2). We won the league and beat Calgary to clinch the championship and ended up with a nice overall record counting tournaments and exhibitions (48–14).

Except for that incident at Medicine Hat, it was a great summer. I made a lot of long-lasting friends up there. Luckily, Dick and I spent just one night at the YMCA. We moved to a boardinghouse with some other guys on the team. It was Ma Fisher's Hungarian boardinghouse and mostly had Hungarian refugees. We were the only Americans, four of us from the team: Creighton, me, Brack Bailey, and Larry Koentopp, who became Gonzaga's baseball coach and athletic director and later bought into the Spokane Indians, the Triple A team of the Seattle Mariners. After the Mount St. Helens eruption in 1980, the

Spokane team took a hit financially, and Larry Koentopp moved it to Las Vegas a couple of years later, where they became the Stars, the first Triple A team in Vegas. Now, because the Oakland Coliseum was being renovated with the Raiders coming back, we had to open our 1996 A's season in Vegas at Cashman Field, the same ballpark used by Larry Koentopp's Stars. He had sold the team a few years earlier to Mandalay Sports Entertainment.

Chapter 13

How Baseball Helped Create a Friendship with Wayne Newton

A FEW YEARS BEFORE I PLAYED for Gary Kirk's Lethbridge White Sox, Gary met Wayne Newton, and they became the best of friends. I got to know Wayne well too, and thanks to Gary, I spent time with Wayne—Mr. Las Vegas.

Gary met Wayne in a Vancouver nightclub, and they hit it off. This was before Wayne Newton was Wayne Newton. Gary went to quite a few lounge shows and sat in the first row, and Wayne would invite him backstage. They got so close that Wayne had Gary serve as best man at his wedding, did a couple of benefit concerts in Lethbridge, and brought Gary and Gary's wife, Loreen, to dine with President Reagan at the White House.

"From all the years I spent in the lounges, one thing I learned to do is read the people in the audience. Gary came to a show once, and then he came back the next night and the next night.

So I said to the maître d', 'Who's the gentleman who keeps coming to my show? I'd like to meet him.' Well, Gary had that perverted sense of humor, so it was easy to get to know him. We became lifelong friends. Gary had four really special friends who shared his sense of humor and looked forward to hanging with him, including [me,] Steve Schott and two Canadian people, Al Foder and Derik Stimson. Steve and Gary teased each other. Steve would rag on Gary, and Gary loved every minute of it.

"Many times Steve and his beautiful wife, Pat, would come to Vegas and check in to one of the major hotels, and Gary would gamble with him but knew I didn't gamble that way. I had owned two casinos, and I never bet the tables or slot machines. One time, we were having dinner, and Gary looked at Steve and said, 'Hey, can you spot me 20 grand?' Steve said, 'Sure, Gary, what do you need it for?' Gary said, 'I'm just going to go play a little bit.' He got up from the table, took Steve's 20 grand, came back a half hour or forty-five minutes later, handed him his 20 grand, and said, 'I had a good day. I won 50.' Steve said, 'Where's my take?' Gary said, 'You got it. I gave it back to you.' It was so funny. He didn't talk a lot about any losses. But Steve is a terrific guy and a great friend of Gary. Gary loved him a lot. They had their baseball connection, but I didn't get into baseball, only because I've worked my whole life. Usually that was at night. I started at the age of 15 going six nights a week, and I'd go to sleep the day I had off. So I never had a chance to truly get involved with baseball or football or even hockey, at least until the Golden Knights came to Las Vegas."

—Wayne Newton

About 20 years after I played in Lethbridge, I went back. I always had fond memories of the town and playing for Gary's team, so I went back and looked him up. I walked in a bank and asked where I might find him, and they directed me to one of the tire shops he ran. He ran a successful tire company in the area. When I met up with him, he looked at me and right away pulled out the team picture of the 1959 Lethbridge White Sox. He had it right there with him. We went out to dinner and caught up. I'm glad I went back and saw him.

When the A's were playing those games in Las Vegas in 1996, Gary would come. He was in Vegas a lot and one time won $100,000 at blackjack somehow, and wanted to bring it back to Canada. So he told me he had made a mistake and didn't get a ticket for his winnings, just walked out with the cash. I told him he couldn't take all that money to Canada; they might think it was drug money or something, or that he had robbed a bank. That's a lot of money to be carrying around. He asked if I could help get him a cashier's check, and I said that would not be easy either. I talked with my financial guy to connect with someone from Bank of America for a favor, and Gary was able to get to see someone at a Las Vegas branch to take care of it. He was impressed and, after that, thought I was somebody really special. He thought I had some pull. It was kind of funny.

"Steve told me he always appreciated what I did for him when he was a young kid. One time, he invites me and my wife to Palm Springs. A few months later, he gives me a call and says he bought the Oakland A's and asks me to join him for a game in Toronto. On his plane. We also went to Montreal because his wife had never been to Montreal.

"Another time the phone rings; it's Steve Schott. He invites me to a game in Oakland. He phones back and says, 'Bring extra clothes because you're going to New York too.' It was an A's-Yankees playoff series. It happened two years in a row. The second time in New York, we partied at some steak house. Everybody knew Steve because he owned the A's. The next day, we come out of an Italian restaurant, and there are two limousines, two patrol cars, and two motorcyclists waiting to give us a police escort to the ballgame. The sirens are going off all the way to Yankee Stadium. Only in New York City. Unbelievable

for a little country kid like me doing this sort of thing. Steve did so much for me. It's unbelievable to see a man go out of his way that much. I've had a wonderful life because of Steve Schott and all my friends I have."

—Gary Kirk

I went back to Lethbridge again for a baseball reunion in 2000 and saw Gary and a lot of guys from the White Sox, including Ray Washburn. Through Gary, I got to know Wayne, and we were fortunate to attend a half dozen of his shows. Wayne helped put Las Vegas on the map, one of the first major entertainers to put Vegas in the headlines. He's still such a great entertainer, and it's so enjoyable to see him in person. "Danke Schoen," "Red Roses for a Blue Lady," on and on. His endurance is amazing, and he was so hospitable and gave us a nice introduction. We went to his place in Las Vegas, the beautiful 40-acre spread, Casa de Shenandoah, a few miles from the strip, where he had a ranch and a lot of horses and other animals before he sold it. His wife, Kat, helps with the business and keeps him going. I got to know her when I flew her and Wayne to Hawaii. By the way, that's a nice story Wayne tells about me pulling 20 grand out of my pocket for Gary, but it might've been closer to a couple of hundred dollars. My limit is usually 10 bucks. I'm not a big gambler. I do it for the fun of it, the challenge. The point is, we always had a great time together with Gary and Wayne and our wives, always a lot of laughs.

"There isn't a day that goes by—and I know this might sound corny, but it's from my heart to yours—that I don't think about Gary and he doesn't cross my mind. He will forever be remembered for as long as I'm walking around. There's no one in my life that even came close to the friendship we had. Gary's favorite song was a hit by Sammy Davis Jr. called 'I've Gotta Be Me.' I had recorded the song on an album, and I gave Gary the album, and

*he came back and said, 'I like your version better than Sammy's.'
I said, 'Then this will be your song from now on.' And it was. Any
time he came to the show, he always wanted to hear 'I've Gotta
Be Me.' His wife had the same kind of sense of humor. When I
was getting married, I asked that my best man wear a tuxedo.
Gary didn't own one. So he was in Vegas, and he and his wife
went into a place to rent tuxedos. Loreen told him he might as
well buy it, and Gary said, 'Oh, I'm never going to use it again,'
and she said, 'Yes, you will. I'll bury you in it.'"*

—Wayne Newton

When Lethbridge had a big party for Gary in 2010 and he was
named Man of the Year and given the key to the city, I flew Wayne
and some of Gary's friends from Nevada to the dinner. It was a great
event, a lot of fun. It was nice to experience their great relationship,
something I never would have known about if, as a kid, I hadn't taken
that 40-hour bus ride to Canada.

Chapter 14

Pro Ball Dreams

IT WAS COLD AND WINDY at Washington Park, a city-owned field south of Santa Clara University, and I was asked by my coach to pitch in relief. It was late in my senior year, and we had to beat St. Mary's to win the conference title. I never was a good reliever. I took a long time to get loose before starts, maybe throwing for 15 minutes. The coach told me to go warm up. I had trouble getting loose in the cold and threw only 10 pitches and felt a pull in my shoulder. Again.

I was hoping it wasn't the same thing as in high school. I went out and pitched and indeed it was the same. The rest of the season, I wasn't worth a damn. I pitched like a 45-year-old. Nothing on the fastball, just threw junk up there.

I was really devastated. Word got out that my arm was bad. The scouts knew. This was 1960, five years before Major League Baseball had its first amateur draft, so the only way for college or high school kids to turn pro was to get scouted and signed. I had heard from enough scouts to believe I could pitch in pro ball, but I had promised my parents I wouldn't sign until I graduated from college. It's funny. My mother was very religious and always worried something would happen to me if I played pro ball. She didn't want me to go on the road with a bunch of drunkards.

I loved baseball. Loved playing, loved pitching. My goal was to turn pro. Some of the guys I competed against were in the major leagues. But when I hurt my arm for a second time, I got disillusioned. I saw others go into the pros, making me think, "Shucks, I could've made it." Well, I don't know if I could have. Dick Creighton signed with the Washington Senators. He didn't throw all that hard, but back then, you didn't have to throw hard. The hardest I threw might have been 92 mph. At least that's what some scout said he had me at.

"I think Steve could've turned pro if healthy. He wasn't the same as a senior that he was as a junior with the shoulder hurting him. Otherwise he probably would've played pro ball. The scouts had been following him for a long time. He was pretty tight with scouts because he had a hell of a career at Bellarmine and carried it to Santa Clara."

—Dick Creighton

So I'm thinking, if I've got a sore arm, if I'm not fully healthy, how am I going to perform and move up the ladder in an organization? I could have tried to play a little ball, but if my arm didn't hold up, where would I be? It could have healed over a period of time, but who knows? I'm not using it as an excuse. I might not have made it at all. Who knows? I didn't think I had the physical attributes at that point to pursue a career and be competitive with an arm that wasn't 100 percent. I just didn't think it would be up to par. I didn't believe surgery was an option. Back then, it was uncharted territory. You were like a guinea pig. It was the kiss of death. I eventually said the heck with it and gave it up.

My baseball career was over, and I was depressed for two or three weeks. But I didn't want to spend my life debating whether I should have played pro ball or not. If I had spent all my time worrying about what I could have done if healthy, I wouldn't be where I am today. I could have sat around and cried about it forever. Instead, I told myself, "I've got to change my way. If something's not working out, I've got to buckle down, find a different path, and figure out what to do with the rest of my life." I knew I wanted to do something that would make money and be successful at it. At the time, I didn't exactly know how to do it.

I came back to Santa Clara for one more semester to get my marketing degree in January 1961: a bachelor of science in commerce from the business school. I was giving up baseball and moving on to the business world. At least until a few years later.

My father-in-law, Joe Sunseri, who helped form the San Jose Bees, convinced me to come out and throw batting practice to these guys. It was 1965, Class C ball, in the California League, and this was an affiliate of the Angels, who were an American League expansion team in 1961 owned by Gene Autry. Back then, there was Class D, Class C, Class B, Class A, Double A, and Triple A. Joe said he had been talking to the Angels about me and arranged for a tryout, though a lot of time had passed since I had pitched or thought of pro ball. My hopes were shattered, and I had shaken it off. But I still had a bad taste in my mouth not being able to turn pro. So I went.

Over the years, San Jose had a number of minor league teams with different affiliations. When I was in high school, the San Jose Red Sox were in the Boston Red Sox's system, and Marty Keough and Albie Pearson got their long careers started in San Jose. Then they became the San Jose JoSox for a couple of years before they were renamed the San Jose Pirates, a farm team of the Pittsburgh Pirates, who moved them to Las Vegas. Joe helped start the San Jose Bees in 1962, and the general manager was Jack Quinn, whose family goes back generations in baseball (my wife, Pat, was his secretary), and his brother, Bob, was the Giants' GM in the 1990s.

The Angels' local scout was at the field: Joe Gordon, a Hall of Fame second baseman who brought others in the organization to look at me. They said go all out and throw as hard as you can, and I did that. "Here goes. Let's see what happens." I was surprised. I didn't think my arm would feel that good. These guys were there for batting practice and thought I was just out there to throw to them, but I'm throwing as hard as I could, getting pitches by them. The Angels were impressed, and I was told I could get a $20,000 bonus and start somewhere in the minor leagues. I did pretty well for them to offer a contract.

Well, I didn't have confidence in my arm. If I had injured it twice, I could injure it another time. I think I was influenced by my friend Dick Creighton, who signed with the Washington Senators and did well in the minors but wasn't given much of a chance. Plus, Pat and I had gotten married in September 1962, and 10 months later had a child, Lisa, and were expecting another child, Steve. Pursuing a baseball career was not in my or my wife's best interests. Too much time had elapsed. It was a nice opportunity, but I couldn't start all over again, couldn't go out on the road and play ball. I had a family now and a different career that was better suited for me.

It didn't take a long time to think about it. I knew I was choosing the right career path. You never know what's in store. You've got to have some guts, stamina, and luck. You've got to have determination and drive, and you've got to be optimistic things will work out.

People ask if I was ever interested in other endeavors, such as coaching. Well, when I was in my early 20s, I tried coaching. I played semipro ball nights and got to know a bunch of the old-time pros who talked me into coaching youth baseball. I wound up coaching Pony League and Pony Colt League, which came right after Little League, so these kids were 13 and 14 years old. I came from work in Milpitas to Santa Clara, and sometimes I cut it close, so Pat, then my fiancée, would bring the equipment.

I enjoyed it. I loved to win, but a lot of times I had to restrain myself from yelling at the umpire or challenging calls. I got to know the umpires well because we went out to have a beer afterward, and they'd say, "Take it easy; it doesn't matter." I said, "Sure it does. I want these kids to win." At the time, people said I should get a teaching credential and coach. A lot of parents tried to talk me into it. But I gave up coaching, at least until my kids got old enough to play sports, and then I coached some basketball and soccer. By then I was dedicated to a business career, but I'll never forget the St. Simon eighth-grade girls basketball team (with my daughter, Kristen) that I coached with Mike Carter. We played in the championship game, and Mike's wife, Trudy, presented roses to all the girls right before the game. They went out and won the league title and were as excited as if they had won a world championship.

If I was going to play any ball, it would be just for fun, and that's what I did after I met a fellow named Chuck Geschke when our kids were in grammar school. We became good friends. He asked if I wanted to join him in pickup basketball Wednesday nights at a gym in Palo Alto, and we'd drive together from Los Altos and show up and play nonstop. We spent a lot of time talking about our dreams. Well, he was the one who created the software company Adobe Inc. and helped invent PDF technology, partnering with John Warnock. I didn't have any clue he'd be that successful. When we were young, the high-tech industry hadn't hit it big yet. We were just dreamers.

Part Three

BUILDING THE A's

Chapter 15

It All Began with an NFL Expansion Bid

I NEVER COULD HAVE IMAGINED buying a professional sports team. Who would? But the possibility popped up a few years before I was asked to purchase the A's. I became part of a group trying to place and own an NFL expansion team in Oakland.

The Raiders had gone to Los Angeles, and the powers that be in Oakland had serious conversations about bringing football back to the East Bay. The 49ers were in San Francisco, and two teams had done well in the Bay Area before the Raiders departed.

I was asked to be part of the plans because they knew I was a sports guy. I had blocks of tickets with the Giants and 49ers. I date back to the Giants arriving as the first major league team in the area and the 49ers the first NFL team. I was a fan of both and had a suite for both at Candlestick Park.

The effort for an expansion team to replace the Raiders came in the early 1990s. We all knew Oakland was a good city and good place for football. There was going to be community support. The team was going to play at the Coliseum, and we thought the NFL was taking us seriously. George Vukasin was the president of the Coliseum board and put together our group, called the East Bay Expansion Group. He asked me and Ed Heafey, an attorney who graduated from Santa Clara, to join and asked me to be majority owner. The four-person group included another attorney, Joe Cotchett, and Ed DeSilva. We tried to lobby the NFL for about a year and a half. When the league had owners' meetings, we'd go along.

One of the meetings was in Arizona, and I'll never forget it. League officials tried to be hospitable to their guests and arranged a doubles tennis match with me and Ed Heafey against Bart Starr and another guy. I was playing tennis with the great Bart Starr—the NFL was trying to get him involved with one of the expansion teams. The match was close, and we actually won, but it didn't matter. I had a situation that came up. A ball was hit right to me at the net, and I just reacted as quickly as I could, used my reflex, and slammed it back. Bart was playing up at the net like I was, and the ball hit him right in the nuts. He doubled over in pain and lost his breath for a moment. Here was Bart Starr, the Hall of Fame quarterback of the Green Bay Packers, and I took him out. I was embarrassed and felt bad hitting the ball in that one spot. He recuperated, fortunately.

Anyway, we didn't get the expansion team. Oakland got shut down. They whittled it down to seven candidates and then eliminated Oakland and Sacramento. That left Jacksonville, Charlotte, Memphis, Baltimore, and St. Louis. Ultimately, in that round of expansion, they picked Jacksonville (Jaguars) and Charlotte (Carolina Panthers).

"We felt very good about our proposal. We presented a package to the NFL which would have been in the upper 10 percent in the league in money given to visiting teams. We had a great owner

in Steve Schott of Citation Builders, one of the top construction firms in Northern California, a man who is exactly the type of owner the NFL is looking for: a solid citizen with no skeletons in his closet. We had a proven record of supporting a team, from the time when the Raiders were here. We had a program that would have given a percentage of our profits to schools. None of these things were acknowledged when they told us that we had been dropped from the expansion list. They just told us we were dropped without any real explanation."

—George Vukasin,
former Oakland Coliseum board president

I found out later from Carmen Policy, who was on the NFL's finance committee, which handled expansion decisions, that the NFL was never going to allow an expansion team in Oakland. He said that would have given California too many teams and that the media coverage and TV contracts would be much more plentiful for the league if teams were more spread out—even though the Bay Area was a bigger market than Jacksonville and Charlotte.

California already had the 49ers in San Francisco, the Rams and Raiders in L.A., and the Chargers in San Diego. We had spent a long time lobbying for a team, and it never worked out. Carmen could have told us from the start, but he really didn't want another team in the Bay Area anyway because he was working for the 49ers as the right-hand man to Eddie DeBartolo as the president and CEO who played a role in all those Super Bowl championships. As a 49ers guy, why would Carmen want competition from Oakland?

The Jacksonville and Carolina teams made their NFL debuts in 1995. As for the folks in Oakland, they got their team. The Raiders returned the same year, which wasn't good news for the A's, while the

Rams moved to St. Louis. California was down to three football teams with none in L.A.

Vukasin and Jim Vohs were the main people who recruited Ken Hofmann and me to buy the A's from the Haas family. Jim was CEO of Kaiser Foundation Hospitals and on the Coliseum board, and I really liked him. He sent me a nice letter after we sold the team in 2005 calling our business model "a resolute, cost-effective and successful management style that is without peer in professional sports." Anyway, Jim, George, and other East Bay officials handpicked Ken and me. They wanted local buyers. Ken was older than I was by 15 or 16 years and said he'd be interested if he had somebody younger to be the lead guy. They knew me from my role with the NFL expansion pursuit and asked Hofmann, "How about Steve Schott?" And he said OK. They asked me, and the arrangement was fine because I'd go in only as the managing partner.

> "In some cases, Steve and Ken saved the team. They don't ever get credit for that, which is somewhat unfair. No matter who would've followed the Haases, it was a tough time to inherit the team. If they didn't save the team, the A's were going somewhere else. I think Steve was unfairly demonized. People didn't realize he was the guy who put the money up, he and Ken."
>
> —Billy Beane

We knew it would be an exciting challenge but stressful. Hofmann had been a minority owner of the Seattle Seahawks, but I didn't have experience running a sports team and was getting consultation from Ed Alvarez, who had been with the 49ers and assisted me at my company. He helped negotiate the deal. We bought the team for $85 million, and $13 million in deferred salaries, and took a loan out at Bank of America to fund the transaction and later paid it off.

I always did like the A's and had gone to games because I was connected in the East Bay through homebuilding. Hofmann and I agreed we wouldn't relocate the A's out of the Bay Area—that was never what we wanted—but Coliseum board members made it very difficult on us, and there was a period of time by virtue of our lease when they threatened to reject us as owners and force us to sell if they didn't think we were qualified to run the team at the Coliseum. Other potential buyers were making waves. There was much to deal with, and I was fully vested in my business, but we took it on, did the best we could—sometimes under grim circumstances—and assured the A's never left the Bay Area on our watch.

Chapter 16

Setting the Budget

ONE OF THE FIRST THINGS I did after buying the A's was ask for a budget. I was totally blown away with the response.

The Haas family, which had bought the A's from Charlie Finley in 1980 for $12.7 million, did a great job running the team, did a lot of positive things, and spent a lot of money, but I honestly have to say I was shocked my first day when the department heads were asked to submit their budgets for the year. I needed to know what we could spend and had Ed Alvarez, our attorney, do the legwork. They came back one by one and said they hadn't submitted traditional budgets. They said they called the Haas family and asked for money. I couldn't imagine running a business without specific budgets. I said we'd need budgets and asked for them to be submitted by the end of the week.

I didn't personally do the due diligence during the purchase. It was done by various groups over six months. I had assumed the budgets were part of it. So now every department had a budget, which was new to some people. I had someone provide a model budget, like in Econ 101, which I did very poorly in. We got through it. I have to say, nobody really complained once the budgets were set. Granted, they were small. The way it had to work was, if you didn't like the budget, you didn't have to stay. If we couldn't all work together at that number, we shouldn't all be there. I didn't really come out and say it that way. They knew that's what I wanted. I don't remember anyone quitting because we were setting budgets. I was glad about that. They agreed to work together. Marketing, sales, accounting, payroll, on and on. Concessions were different. They were dealt out to someone else, Jim Wilson. We had to follow the rules, and that's to set budgets ahead of time.

Along with then-GM Sandy Alderson, we agreed to the number we could spend in baseball operations each year. So much on the salaries, so much on the draft, so much on the farm system. It came together, and Billy Beane bought into it when he came on board. I wasn't excited about the amount of money I was spending, because maybe I didn't think it was enough, but it was all we had to run the show. A big payroll isn't the only way to be a winner or playoff team. We showed that. Now, if we got close to the playoffs and needed to spend money late in the season that exceeded the budget, and I thought it was prudent for the team, we'd find a way to get an extra million or a couple of million. We had a little money set aside as a contingency, and we could go over budget because we knew we had a little playoff money coming in from the postseason.

We weren't in it to make money, however. We were in it to save the team from leaving. You've got to remember this: I acquired the team from one of the biggest spenders in baseball, and I came in from a business background in which everything had to be done carefully with how you spend, trying to make every decision count and trying to avoid big mistakes. That's how I was brought up in my world. It was a difference of night and day in ownership.

"That trickled down all the way to the grounds crew. We always had a budget but not necessarily the detail of budgets the

new owners were used to. Previously, we did do budgets and spreadsheets, but it was, 'If you go over here, you can take from there.' It wasn't as streamlined. I never felt under the Haas family it was a free-for-all, but there was more maneuverability. So it was just a little bit different concept. I had just recently graduated from Arizona State's business school and knew some people were OK with it, but for others, it was a little bit of a culture shock.

"Something else changed for us under Mr. Schott and Mr. Hofmann: My crew had been Alameda County employees, and now they were going to be A's employees. That came from Ed Alvarez. We brought it in-house and took a little more control of the situation, giving us more skin in the game. Not only us, but the whole organization became more streamlined and detail-oriented."

—Clay Wood, A's head groundskeeper

I knew we needed talent on the field, and we had good drafts and acquired good pitching. That was the key. That's how we became successful. We picked up players off the waiver wire and free agents— not always what you call the A players but the B players. We had some weaknesses but a strong rotation. Everything had to work out right. I'll tell you what—there's something to be said for a $200 million payroll, which doesn't guarantee a winner, but there's also something to be said for getting on the bandwagon and working together and doing all we can with the resources budgeted and getting the right players and giving them a chance, and that's what we did very well.

Chapter 17

The Raiders and the Horror That Is Mount Davis

WHEN WE BOUGHT THE A's, there was never a serious consideration the Raiders would return to Oakland. We had the Coliseum to ourselves, and I planned to make the stadium more baseball friendly, as the Angels did with Anaheim Stadium over the years. We wanted to modify it to our liking.

The Coliseum opened in 1966 when the Raiders moved in, and the A's arrived from Kansas City two years later. Anaheim Stadium also opened in 1966, and it is hard to imagine considering the difference between the two facilities now. In the late 1990s, $118 million was spent on improving Anaheim Stadium. In Oakland, I would have spent $50 million on upgrading the Coliseum if the city and county had matched it to make it more user-friendly. It was easier in those days to finance ballparks both privately and publicly, and it was a good possibility we could have made it work at the Coliseum and adapted it more for baseball.

Then the bomb dropped. The Raiders were coming back after playing in Los Angeles from 1982 to 1994 and reconstructing the Coliseum.

Long Schott

The agreement called for expansion of a giant seating structure in center field, which became known as Mount Davis, a tribute to Al Davis. It enclosed the stadium and wiped out the view of the Oakland hills, which had been part of the ambiance for decades. Before Mount Davis, the Coliseum was better than Candlestick Park for baseball. Another 20,000 seats might have helped for football, but it hurt for baseball. All those seats were useless unless a team such as the Yankees came to town or we were in the playoffs and we'd draw well more than 50,000. But sometimes during the week, we'd have 8,000 or 10,000. Without Mount Davis, that monstrosity, we would have been fine.

We were recruited to buy the A's, and behind our backs, the city and county went out and courted the Raiders. We didn't know about the deal until the news broke. I wasn't happy about it. Nobody had showed us any plans about redoing the Coliseum. They kind of did a number on us, keeping it a secret from Ken Hofmann and me. They knew we'd put up a roadblock if we knew the stadium was going to change the way it did.

Yes, there were rumors of a Raiders return, which were universally hard to believe because football teams back then just didn't leave and return to their original site, and the Raiders were the only team in Los Angeles and being wooed by a potential Hollywood Park stadium deal. I remember Ed DeSilva, who spearheaded the Raiders' return, called me one day and asked if I would care if the Raiders came back to the Bay Area. I had no clue they were considering redoing the Coliseum, and I didn't put up a big fight because there was never any dialogue about how a Raiders renovation would affect the A's.

When we bought the A's, we had all these guys on the Coliseum board on our side. They said, "We're behind you 100 percent. We've got your back. Don't worry. You're going to be fine here." Lo and behold, what did they do right after they signed us up? They brought the Raiders back and ruined the Coliseum. It didn't turn out well for us. You'd think after all this, the people on the joint committee would be our best friends and do all they could to help, but they avoided us. I don't mean to complain, but the last thing we needed was for the Raiders to come back. The plans weren't disclosed to us until after Al Davis signed the deal in June 1995. It was approved the following month, and the Raiders would play in Oakland that fall. We had reached an agreement to buy the A's in January 1995 and closed on the deal in November. We stuck with it. We had every right to sue, but the last thing new owners needed was filing a lawsuit, getting tied up in court, and spending millions on legal bills. More than anything, we wanted to make it work. We wanted the A's to stay in the area.

"We were a gnat on an elephant's ass. In the beginning, there was no talk of the Raiders. Then the Raiders came, and they wanted us to leave. The politicians just weren't supportive. They talked a big game, but when it came down to it, they didn't do anything to help us. It was frustrating. Steve and Ken could have said forget it and walked away. They didn't."

—Nick Rossi, attorney for the A's and co-owner Ken Hofmann

It couldn't have gone much worse for us at the start. We never had a chance to implement our upgrades for baseball. Our first season of ownership was 1996, and instead of celebrating our Opening Day at the Coliseum, we had to pack up and open the season in Las Vegas at Cashman Field, a little minor league park. Why? Because the Coliseum was under construction. Mount Davis was being built for the start of the NFL season, which would come in September. All that money was spent to build up the Coliseum for the Raiders, who put that debt against the city and county, and taxpayers are still paying it off even though the team now makes its home in Las Vegas.

Long Schott

So it was a bad situation. The Raiders screwed us royally from day one. They tore up the field every year. It was a mess. The last two months of the baseball season, we had to deal with it, and Clay Wood, our excellent head groundskeeper, did a very nice job all things considered. If we had known when we were being recruited to buy the A's that the Raiders were coming back, we definitely wouldn't have bought the team. I wouldn't have gone in, and Ken Hofmann wouldn't have either. On the other hand, had the Raiders never come back to Oakland, it would have been a lot easier on the A's. We could have done a lot more things with the stadium and the team, but we always were hamstrung because of the Raiders.

We would have loved for it to be an exciting time in franchise history, but we couldn't open the season in our own stadium. I was not about to let it be opened to the public and have people get hurt during construction. It was far from finished. We absolutely had to go to Las Vegas for our first six games. I remember Sandy Alderson came up with the idea. There was nowhere else to play.

"The Coliseum was a beautiful baseball park that people enjoyed going to and was so much nicer than Candlestick. Then the Raiders came back, and Schott was saddled with the Mount Davis situation. So he began his ownership tenure with his first games at Vegas, which was just awful. When the A's returned to Oakland, construction was ongoing during day games, with drilling and jackhammering up there. C'mon. The bleachers, the most popular part of the ballpark, were all gone. It just killed attendance. Plus it was a bad team, so it was hard to sell tickets anyway. It took winning before you could win the fans back."

—David Feldman, A's historian

It was not an easy situation once the Coliseum was transformed. And remember, this was shortly after the 1994–95 players' strike that wiped out a World Series and led to attendance plunging across baseball. Suddenly, with all those seats, it was hard to sell season tickets when people knew we weren't going to have sellouts. We had to rely on walk-ups, and that was hard to do. We needed to have a big staff in place, with food and beverage and everything, just in case. It wasn't going to be easy anyway, but the Raiders made it extremely difficult.

Chapter 18

Unfortunate Press Briefings

IN HOMEBUILDING, YOU DON'T HAVE MANY press conferences. You'd ask a newspaper to come by your site if you wanted publicity. Or you'd pay for an advertisement. It was about selling houses, not yourself, though a lot of guys in homebuilding wanted to sell themselves, which made me chuckle. I didn't live for that.

After buying the A's, I made two major mistakes in comments to the press. I entered thinking I didn't want to spend money that wasn't mine, and I bit myself on the butt. I said to the press we wanted to win as much as anybody and weren't necessarily in it to make money, but we were not going to spend our own money and lose money, and that shocked people. I told reporters we had to be careful because we didn't want to take a loss financially, like any business. It exploded.

While that's definitely the case with most every team, I shouldn't have said that. Not many owners are going to say they don't mind losing money. Or will take money out of their pocket. My comments didn't come off right. I was criticized for not spending, but I wanted to be frugal while we rebuilt the team through the draft and with younger players. That's what Ken Hofmann and I agreed on, but I'm the one who set the budget.

> *"Steve wasn't a cheapskate. He was a responsible businessman. He realized it was stupid to intentionally lose money. Some in their quest to win deliberately lose money."*
>
> —Jerry Reinsdorf, Chicago White Sox owner

Another mistake was a comment I made about Terry Steinbach, our catcher from the three World Series teams. I was asked what I thought of the salaries of players. I grew up when we thought a .300 batting average was the gold standard for a hitter. That was our rule of thumb. I questioned whether Terry was worth what he was making. I didn't mean to pick on him. I know catchers don't always hit .300 unless you're a young Yogi Berra. The press jumped all over me. I never should have gotten involved in a conversation like that and subsequently apologized to Terry.

That was my first press conference. It was a learning process. I had nobody to help me on that front, and sometimes I was too damn honest. It got to the point where I didn't want to say anything to anybody in the press. That was before I met Sam Spear, the longtime media relations director at Golden Gate Fields racetrack who knew the ins and outs in baseball and was media savvy.

Sam was referred to me by a personal friend, Jim Conn, who went to school with me at Santa Clara and was the president at the old Bay Meadows racetrack. Jim called and said he thought he had a guy who could help me. I didn't know Sam but had lunch with him and said let's try it out. I really loved having Sam around. He had a good rapport with the press and set up lunches with me. Did it help? Somewhat. But a lot of them didn't change their opinion of me.

> *"I was interested as a baseball purist and someone with a deep love of the game, and I also knew media relations with a lot of contacts in the industry. I worked for Bob Lurie of the Giants for a short period of time and had good relationships with many managers: Earl Weaver, Frank Robinson, Dick Williams, Alvin Dark, Bill Rigney, Joe Altobelli, Jim Davenport, Wes Westrum, Charlie Fox, Darrell Johnson. I thought I could help Steve because I've been involved in radio, TV, and newspapers for many years and just thought my expertise and relationships with the media could be helpful to him. A lot of positive things happened in my time with Steve Schott, and I wish it lasted longer. We were able to help turn around his relationship with the media and put a better face on the ownership of the franchise, and he started enjoying it more. I worked on changing his image and wanted the media to realize he's just a regular person."*
>
> —Sam Spear

If Sam were around from the beginning, I think we could have had better relationships because he could have told me a little more about what I could do or should do. We would have had a different approach, a different ballgame. I don't know if I was cut out to be an owner, but once I got into it, I wanted to be successful. I've always been a winner or tried to be a winner, like with anything in life or business.

Chapter 19

Baseball's Owners

I REMEMBER MY FIRST OWNERS' MEETING. I was the new guy and didn't know everything. We had to vote on cosigning a note for the Milwaukee Brewers. Bud Selig owned the Brewers and wasn't commissioner yet, and George Steinbrenner put the motion up for a vote.

I was shocked. I wondered why I should be mortgaging my own team and figured Bud could do what he had to do without collateralization of all the teams. He was trying to build a new stadium at that point. Well, I was in the minority. I abstained and surprised everybody. He got it through unanimously.

Owners' meetings weren't too exciting. In fact, they were sometimes pretty boring, to be honest. Bud would talk, and guys would detail their reports from different committees. I came aboard right after the 1994–95 players' strike, and many teams were experiencing some real financial squeezes, including ours. There was no real revenue sharing when I first got there. The only revenue sharing was receiving a little bit of the gate when teams played road games. That was old school. You couldn't exist on that. No team wanted to come to Oakland because the gate often wasn't enough to capitalize.

Long Schott

"Right after Steve and Ken Hofmann took over, I asked Sandy Alderson how they were received at the owners' meetings, and Sandy said, 'Very well.' He thought the other owners admired them because they were both self-made. They didn't inherit the money."

—Steve Vucinich, A's longtime equipment manager

The meetings didn't really pick up until we started talking about interleague play and new things coming into the game. Interleague play started in 1997, which arrived two years after the advent of the wild card, which I thought was a tremendous idea and brought more excitement to more teams. There were four playoff teams in each league instead of two, and an extra layer of playoffs. The 1998 season brought two expansion teams in Arizona and Tampa Bay, and we were up to 30 teams. That was the year the Brewers moved to the National League.

There wasn't much to cheer about in those years beyond Cal Ripken Jr. breaking the ironman record for most consecutive games played. That was before the home run chase in 1998 with Mark McGwire and Sammy Sosa and the ensuing steroid issues. Jose Canseco wrote the books. Barry Bonds broke the records. I didn't know McGwire was taking that stuff. I had heard whispers about Canseco. We found out about Jason Giambi after he left. I didn't have a clue it was going on like it was. There was no real testing when we owned the team. The feeling was steroids weren't banned from the game. There were federal laws against illegal steroids, but people in baseball felt there was nothing preventing them from taking steroids because the game didn't have any strong rules against them. Now we know steroids were widespread with most every team.

At the owners' meetings, George Steinbrenner usually had the most to say, the most dominant presence. When he wanted to make a point, he was heard. As were Jerry Reinsdorf and Eddie Einhorn, the White Sox and the Red Sox owners. Bud had certain guys in his corner, including Steinbrenner and Reinsdorf. Sometimes the trouble with Bud was, you didn't always know if an answer was definitive or not because someone could sway him in a different direction. He tried to please everybody.

I wasn't very vocal at the meetings. I was busy trying to keep my business going and didn't have time to get involved in a lot of committees. A lot of other owners, running their baseball teams is all they did. I had department heads with the A's running the team, but I still tried to be on hand. I'd be at my business in the morning and helicopter to the Coliseum for the game.

I got to know Steinbrenner pretty well and can't say anything bad about him. Even though he might have had a reputation for being a wild man, he was very decent to me. When I sat with George at A's-Yankees games, he always was a gentleman. Reinsdorf was very gracious and one time wanted to have one of his top guys, Ron Schueler, the general manager who previously worked for the A's, take my grandson, Michael, who was 3 or 4, around the park in Chicago and give him some White Sox souvenirs, but my grandson refused because it wasn't A's gear. Completely shot him down. It wasn't green and gold. He liked the A's and didn't care about the White Sox. I was a little embarrassed, but it was cute.

Jerry liked to sit around after meetings, maybe go out for dinner and drinks, and he always had good stories. He told me he thought it was a mistake to fire Tony La Russa in the 1980s, so I wasn't surprised when he rehired Tony in 2021 even though it took him a long time to get that opportunity. Jerry and some of the owners would have cocktail hour the first night of the meetings, and he and maybe a half dozen others would go for drinks and invite me, and I looked forward to that. That's how I got to know them well. I wouldn't have gotten to otherwise. That was fun just shooting the breeze with those guys.

"At owners' meetings, we'd usually all go out to dinner one night, and after dinner, we'd hang out, smoke cigars, and tell jokes. I recall Steve sometimes joining us. Steve was a good owner, a very intelligent fellow. Most of the time, we agreed on issues. I guess you like people who agree with you."

—Jerry Reinsdorf

I got to know Jerry Colangelo, who owned the Diamondbacks, because we were neighbors in Carmel on the Monterey Peninsula, and I thought he was very nice. I thought highly of Carl Pohlad of the Twins, John Harrington of the Red Sox, and Paul Beeston of the Blue Jays, who wrote me a nice letter saying he appreciated how we ran the team.

"You never had to worry about what Steve thought or where he stood. You ask a direct question, you'll get a direct answer. He was going to do it his way and wasn't going to get in a battle with big-market teams. His big goal was to get a new stadium, and he never got there. Coming after the Haases wasn't easy, but he had terrific success. Not all the owners got to know him well, but they respected him and listened to him and knew he was committed to owning an American League team in the Bay Area."

—Paul Beeston, former president and CEO of the Toronto Blue Jays

Arte Moreno of the Angels appreciated the way we did business in Oakland and told me he'd like to model his team after mine, make it an exact replica. He lost track and went the other way, though, and gave huge contracts that didn't work out to Albert Pujols, Josh Hamilton, and others. He broke all his rules.

Before Arte bought the Angels, when they were for sale in the early 2000s, John Henry of the Marlins wanted me to contract the A's and go down and buy the Angels. Henry wanted to partner with me in Anaheim and said he had plenty of money. That was at a time when baseball tried to collapse two teams. This was a few years after Arizona and Tampa Bay were added, giving us 30 teams. Bud wanted to go back to 28, and the big talk was that Montreal and Minnesota were going to lose their franchises. Their finances weren't good, and they had outdated stadiums, like us. The owners wanted to reduce the number of teams by two because they didn't feel there was enough of a market and revenue for 30 teams. They were offering $250 million buyouts. It was not a popular thing. It never happened. Minnesota courts said the Twins had to honor their lease, and the union fought contraction. The teams survived, fortunately. Finances got a lot better. The Twins built a new ballpark, but the Expos never got a park and were relocated to Washington.

Other teams were candidates to fold, including ours. There were owners who thought there were too many teams in California and that it would have been beneficial to just contract the A's. When John Henry asked about getting the A's contracted and making a pitch to run the Angels, he wanted me to run the team in Anaheim because he wanted to stay on the East Coast. I thought that was a compliment. I was flattered. It might have sounded good on paper, but I wouldn't get involved with that. I wasn't going to move down there. Why would I want to be running down there all the time? I didn't want to take that on. If I was going to run a team, I would do it in the Bay Area. We bought the A's to keep them in the area, saving the team from being moved someplace else, not that we got much credit for that.

As it turned out, no team was contracted. John Henry sold the Marlins to Jeffrey Loria and bought into the Red Sox. Loria sold the Expos to Major League Baseball and took over the Marlins. Arte Moreno bought the Angels. We stayed put. There was another reason for not contracting the A's. We were turning it around in Oakland. We were winning more and drawing better. Things were looking brighter.

Chapter 20

Difficult Roster Conversations

MY HOMEBUILDING BUSINESS PREVENTED me from spending all my time with the baseball team. For me, especially if I wasn't always around, it was imperative for all the team's employees to be accountable and face their responsibilities, like in my homebuilding business. I didn't want to interfere with the baseball decisions. I'd ask about a certain play or move, why we started this guy in the playoffs instead of another guy. But every day is a different day, and you can't really nitpick. You don't want to come off saying you know it all, but you know enough not to have the wool pulled over your eyes.

Sometimes Sandy Alderson or Billy Beane would ask my opinion, but I mostly tried to step back from the decision-making process. If they wanted to get rid of guys, it was up to them. When it came to managerial hiring, we usually had discussions about it. In some cases, I just had to speak out if something bothered me enough.

Sandy and Billy made a lot of great transactions that helped us win a lot of games over the years. Not everything worked out. They never do for any team. In fact, I remember I was asked about a player before

I even owned the team. It was before the June 1995 draft, when the sale hadn't yet been made official. We were going to have the fifth overall pick, and I was asked to come watch Ariel Prieto throw. Prieto was a pitcher from Cuba, and we were going to give him a million bucks. They wanted me to give my OK, but what was I going to say when I didn't own the team yet? No? I went down and saw him work out and was stuck between a rock and a hard place. We drafted Prieto, and he didn't pan out. A few picks later, the Rockies took Todd Helton, a great player who might be in the Hall of Fame one day, but you never know with the baseball draft. Things don't always turn out as expected. More than any other sport, it's unpredictable.

Another example: In 1996, the first year we owned the team, it seemed every time I saw Todd Van Poppel pitch, he struggled. Van Poppel was one of four starting pitchers the A's had selected in the first 36 picks of the 1990 draft, and these guys were supposed to help carry the franchise through the decade, but it didn't work out. None stuck around except Van Poppel. I told Sandy I was getting tired of watching it and wanted to send him down to the minors. I wasn't fully familiar yet with the rules back then and asked why we kept pitching him and was told he was out of minor league options.

I was an old pitcher and knew it was important to develop top young pitching, and here was a kid who desperately needed more development. The thing is, he got a major league contract out of the draft even though he was in high school, and that was necessary because otherwise he was going to go pitch in college, at Texas. What that meant was he went on the 40-man roster right away and had to attend big-league training camp. It hurried his clock, and he had to stay in the majors or else be placed on waivers for any team to pick him up. We stuck with Van Poppel a little more, but enough was enough, and we severed ties with him late in the 1996 season.

Then there was Ben Grieve. He was the league's top rookie in 1998, and Billy wanted to sign him long-term. I had reservations and expressed them to Billy. Something didn't sit right with me, including his defense, arm, and base running. He was a second overall draft pick but didn't have an overall game. Billy said Ted Williams couldn't do anything but hit. Come on, you're going to mention Ben Grieve in the same breath as Ted Williams? We gave Grieve a four-year contract for $13 million before the 2000 season. I wasn't all for it. In fact, I said if we were going to give him the extension, we would have to eventually trade him. That kind of pissed off Billy. Well, he wound up playing just one more year in Oakland, and we traded him to Tampa, and it was one of the best things we ever did. It was a three-way deal, and we got Cory Lidle, Johnny Damon, and Mark Ellis, three guys who were a great help in our playoff runs. Lidle made our rotation deeper, Damon was our leadoff hitter, and Ellis was an infield prospect who had a very good career. Grieve's numbers went down after that.

"Grieve hit 28 homers in '99, 27 in 2000. We gave him that extension, which allowed us to trade him after the 2000 season. That was part of the reason. Players had better value when signed through their arbitration years. You had cost certainty, which created more value for good young players. It worked out well because we were able to trade him in the Damon deal. So really, Grieve was in Oakland for three years at a minimum salary, and when we traded him, his contract escalated for the next three years. We got a lot out of him and a lot out of the trade. As for Prieto, if we're here to debate whether he was a good selection or not, I'm here to say not so much. Grady Fuson and the staff wanted Helton. We were so desperate for pitching. It was not necessarily a particularly good decision but a good lesson learned."

—**Billy Beane**

Long Schott

In 2004, we were having a rough time closing games. I was on a trip through St. Louis and Chicago for a stretch of interleague games, and it seemed like every night, we had bullpen problems. I got really upset. It got ridiculous. We won just one game in those cities but could have won more if we had held on to leads. We were floundering. We had Keith Foulke in 2003, and he was magnificent as our closer. We tried Arthur Rhodes and other guys in 2004, including Jim Mecir and Chad Bradford, but couldn't find anyone consistent and couldn't rely on a closer by committee. We had more blown saves than saves, if you can believe it. I said, "We've got to find a closer." You didn't have to be a wizard to realize it, but I really came down hard. Before the trip ended, we had made a trade with Houston for Octavio Dotel, who had plenty of experience in the role and did a good job for us. He saved 22 games down the stretch, and that helped solidify our pitching. We won 91 games but finished a game behind the Angels and missed the playoffs for the first time in a long while, and it made you think about all the games we could have closed out but didn't.

Dotel was eligible for arbitration after the season, and we thought enough of him to give him a contract of nearly $5 million. He was a good pickup, and not just for us. He ended up playing 15 years for a total of 13 teams, then a major league record.

Part Four

THE MONEYBALL YEARS

Chapter 21

The Transition from Sandy Alderson to Billy Beane

SANDY ALDERSON WAS AN INTEGRAL PART of the A's organization and built teams that went to the World Series three years in a row—1988, 1989, and 1990—and was great in assisting with the transition after our purchase.

When I got there, Sandy had a lot on his plate as both general manager and team president, and I was a little surprised he was taking on so much. Other teams had separate departments for the baseball side and the business side. I thought we should split things up. I brought in Ed Alvarez to help run things in business, but he was an attorney and didn't have the business background or characteristics. One of his jobs was to find a marketing director, and we kept coming up with the wrong guys. I found out pretty quickly we were in trouble and told Ed it wasn't working. He moved to Coliseum administration.

Meanwhile, Sandy thought the world of Billy Beane, who was the assistant GM at the time, and was always touting him as being very bright and very good at what he did. I said, "Well, Sandy, if he's as good as you say he is, we should promote him." I asked Sandy about remaining president and handling business and making Billy the GM. After the 1997 season, Billy, who was 35 at the time, took over GM duties and day-to-day responsibilities in the baseball operations department. We were rebuilding. I thought he was the right guy; he definitely was bright and had a lot of energy.

I was just following logic, but I guess I might have stepped on Sandy's domain. I didn't think he'd care. It was a team effort. He didn't debate why he should keep both positions. He didn't disagree with me or question it. I wasn't cutting his salary or anything. But it obviously made him concerned. After the 1998 season, three years after I bought the club and a year after we divided the roles, he left for the commissioner's office. That was a surprise to me that he took the job. It was an offer that came through me, and I ran it by Sandy. He might have thought he was getting pushed out the door. He didn't say that, but it never was my intent to push him out. Deep down, I think Sandy wanted the commissioner's job, and maybe if he went back to New York, he'd have an inside track. There was talk he could be a candidate at some point. If he wanted to move back there in hopes of landing a bigger and better job, that was his decision. I wasn't going to say no. It wasn't a case of Sandy getting squeezed out. When that offer came along from Major League Baseball, he was ready to take it.

"Steve and Ken were a similar type. They weren't sycophants. They both smelled BS. If you BS'd them, they'd catch you in it. Tell them the truth. It was a pretty linear relationship. Steve wasn't warm and fuzzy, but you kind of knew where you stood. When I had more success and felt more sure of myself, we had

plenty of times we didn't agree. 'You hang up on me, I hang up on you.' Next day, we were fine.

"It was very strange after they took over after the 1995 season. There were some draconian cuts. They did a lot of things on the business side that didn't work. The baseball side huddled together and was going to ride it out. Obviously, Sandy was such a great leader that we all loved, and eventually things changed. Sandy was put back as president after six months, deservedly so. Steve reserved the right to change his mind, to his credit. I was elevated to GM. I think Steve ultimately learned to trust Sandy. Then Sandy left for the commissioner's office as the No. 2 guy. I always respected the fact that Steve gave me my first opportunity. He said, 'Hey, here's what you have to work with. I'll basically leave you alone.' He wasn't often in his office. He didn't stay in our hair on a daily basis. That's not a bad environment to be in. Sometimes he did voice his opinion from afar, but we could deal with it."

—Billy Beane

Sandy's absence did leave a void. He didn't give me a lot of notice, and I asked him who he'd recommend to take over his position. He suggested Mike Crowley, who was the controller but hadn't been in the organization very long. He had been a financial guy all his life and was a smart young man. He was local too; his wife had been my daughter's roommate at Santa Clara, and he went to St. Simon grammar school in Los Altos and St. Francis High in Mountain View with my kids. I wasn't sure he was ready to take over, but I had to find somebody pretty quickly. Mike didn't have a lot of experience but filled the shoes and learned well on the job. He was a good hands-on numbers guy but didn't have the marketing background to help us get butts in the seats. I was on him to focus more on marketing. Season tickets were down, and we never really improved on that. It was all about walk-up sales and making sure we had good teams. Our marketing could have been much better.

We never did have a strong marketing department. Not to be critical, but it was hard with that stadium to get a lot of people interested, especially after the Raiders came back. Despite all that, we took over a team following the 1994–95 players' strike and brought it back to the point where we averaged 2.2 million fans over our final four years of ownership, a big jump from 1.1 million in our first year.

"Steve Schott heavily leaned on the experience of Sandy Alderson and Billy Beane and let them do what they do. A lot of new owners wouldn't do that. They'd think they're the smartest guys in the room and great talent evaluators, especially owners with baseball backgrounds. That was the key to the A's being successful again. When Sandy stepped aside, there was never a question Billy would take over. So on the baseball side of things, there was continuity, and what started as a rebuild in Schott's first couple of years had a chance to keep going. It was a deep farm system with Giambi coming up and Tejada and Chavez, and the pitchers, Hudson, Mulder, and Zito, but it really goes to the deals Billy started pulling off at the trade deadline in '99. Picking up Terrence Long and Jason Isringhausen in separate deals with the Mets, Omar Olivares and Randy Velarde from the Angels, and Kevin Appier from the Royals. That set the framework for success in 2000 and beyond. Schott let the baseball people do their baseball people thing."

—David Feldman, A's historian

A few years after Sandy left, we thought Billy was leaving, too, when the Red Sox wanted him to run their team in 2002. They committed to him. He clearly was on his way to Boston, and I had made the decision to promote Paul DePodesta. But Billy got cold feet at the last minute. I was getting back from Sunday mass in Palm Desert, and my wife told me Billy had called, and she said, "You've got to talk to Billy right away because he's pretty emotional." He didn't want to leave his daughter. He wanted to stay here in the worst way and pleaded with me.

"When I decided not to go to Boston, I called up Steve and told him I changed my mind and wanted to stay. I had been pretty much out the door. I think that surprised him, but he was great about it. I'll always appreciate that."

—Billy Beane

I took him back, and that made it very tough on me because I had already told Paul that if Billy left, he'd be the guy. Like I've always said, you make a decision, you stick with it. Paul wasn't so happy about how it turned out. He's not the kind of guy who'd say that, but I could tell. When Billy came back, Paul didn't want a long deal and said, "Mind if I play the year out?" I didn't blame him. He's a good guy and was going to be pursued by other teams. He was that good at what he did.

Frank McCourt had just bought the Dodgers and called to ask for an interview. I told McCourt, "I'll let him out of his deal, but you better pay him a good price." I had Paul's back side, and he deserved it. He got a very good deal. But not before he helped us reach the next level in Oakland.

Chapter 22

The *Moneyball* Book and Movie

I'VE SEEN THE *MONEYBALL* MOVIE pop up on television and gotten so frustrated with the way it was presented, I've turned it off. It was especially unfair to our manager, Art Howe. That's an area where it got carried away. I thought he got a raw deal. The movie exploited him and characterized him unfairly, and they made him look like Humpty Dumpty, which wasn't true at all. No offense to Philip Seymour Hoffman, the actor who played Art.

The first film idea got rejected. Maybe it wasn't Hollywood enough, so they brought in Brad Pitt to play Billy Beane and jazzed it up. It's typical Hollywood, which can be expected, but there were some ridiculous things in the movie that just didn't happen. Such as a Coke machine in the clubhouse. Really? Come on. Nobody charged a dollar for sodas.

"Major League Baseball tried to get them to take that scene out. They had oversight on a few things. They didn't want the club to look cheap. The scene stayed in, but that never happened

that way. Nobody paid for soda. Just like the conversation with Billy and Dave Justice in the batting cage. That never happened either."

—Steve Vucinich, longtime A's equipment manager

It made like I was trying to squeeze blood out of a turnip. Hey, listen, everyone knew what the budget was, and we all went through the budget together and bought into it. We had an understanding. If we were close to the playoffs, we'd get the money somewhere to bring in players. That was part of the deal. It was touched on in the first few minutes of the movie when the guy who played me, Bobby Kotick, and Brad Pitt were in my office talking about the budget and what we needed to do after losing Jason Giambi, our best hitter; Johnny Damon, our leadoff hitter; and Jason Isringhausen, our All-Star closer, to free agency. Remember, Giambi came up through our farm system, and we had converted Isringhausen into a closer, so these players really evolved in great ways with us. The task was to find new players to fill their spots within the budget, and Billy and Paul DePodesta used their smarts and creativity and got it done. That's where Scott Hatteberg and some others entered the picture. It didn't backfire; it worked out. That was the premise of the movie, though I know Art didn't like it.

"That was a disgrace. That was terrible. It was amazing how Paul DePodesta had been with the team a couple of years, and they made it look like it was his first year coming over bringing all this information. Also, that stuff about me asking in a hallway for a longer contract, that was so much baloney. Billy and I had our differences, obviously. I managed the way I felt was best. For example, stealing a base and putting down a bunt. He thought stealing or bunting was giving up an out. He would come down with these statistics saying you could score more with no outs from first than with one out from second. I said it depends on

who's coming up. Bottom of the order, yes. But if your 3, 4, 5 guys are coming up with men in scoring position, I like my chances. He'd use a blanket statement, and I'd debate that. Baseball is situational. It depends on who's at the plate, how many outs there are, who's coming up next. All those things I took into consideration. If you're facing their ace and it's hard to score runs, and you're getting only a few hits, let's hope you get one with a man in scoring position. Billy wasn't big on stolen bases. It made no sense to me, and I'd say there are tremendous percentages of being successful. You take advantage of what the other team is going to give you. If you don't recognize that, you're not going to be successful."

—Art Howe

To me, the beginning of quote-unquote Moneyball to analyze players was a software program Paul DePodesta brought to us in the late 1990s, Advanced Value Matrix, or AVM. Paul and Billy Beane wanted to implement it, and I asked how. They said, "We'd need to sign up by leasing it." I said, "Well, if it's so good, why lease it? Why don't we buy it?" That would give us a great advantage if we were the only team with access. Billy and Paul said a few other teams were using it too. I said we should buy it when the lease was up so we'd have exclusivity. They tried to negotiate, but we couldn't cut a deal. We did have the program locked up for a couple of years with a few other teams.

"It was pretty new, and we did a test run on it and thought it would be a good addition, and Steve was very supportive while other owners probably wouldn't have been."

—Billy Beane

So we moved forward. It provided many of the stats Billy thought were important and allowed him to acquire players who would fit in our budget and be able to perform to the level of players who didn't fit in the budget. All teams have access to that information now, but they didn't so much in the late 1990s and early 2000s. It gave insight into elements of the game that other teams weren't considering. Does it pay to have a runner try to steal third? Sacrifice a guy to second? It broke down the benefit of working a pitcher for a walk, the consequence of striking out versus hitting the ball to the right side. The program examined all these things and provided valuable statistical data. That's a reason we started having guys take so many pitches and be more open to drawing a walk. It got to be the approach through the whole system.

"There was a lot of stuff we pursued, things we considered to be informational advantages at the time. We were keen on making them proprietary for us, and Steve was certainly supportive of those efforts. I would say the 30 teams now have access to an incredible amount of information we didn't have access to in 1999. We were on that road. We definitely wanted it. We knew some of these sources of information could help us with our decision-making. None of them were going to be crystal balls or anything like that, but if it could make us a little bit better, help us get our arms around the general inefficiency in our decision-making, we obviously wanted to pursue it and had Steve's blessing to do so."

—Paul DePodesta

Did I question it? Sure. Did all the advanced information help? To some degree, yes. How much? I don't know. Do I think it makes that much difference whether a guy is taking close pitches or hitting away? I'm not sure. There are reasons guys don't bunt anymore. Or try stealing bases. It's about going with the odds. Shifts work a lot of the time, but I don't see enough people trying to punch it to the opposite side. There are pluses and minuses to everything. I come from an era when you'd go up and hit, not look for a walk, when you'd prefer to make contact and go to right field or punch a base hit. I mean, there were always guys looking to lengthen the count and get on base any way possible, but with the A's, we emphasized it more than any other team as a tactic to win games, and we won a lot of games.

That's what interested Michael Lewis, the *Moneyball* author—the way Billy and the guys were getting more bang for the buck and finding ways with undervalued players to outperform other teams that had far more resources.

> *"Some of the stuff we were doing was new, period. Art had every reason to say, 'What are you guys doing?' In fairness to Art, too, I remember he once said, 'I don't know what the hell you guys are doing up there, but it's working, so I'm going with it.' We were doing things such as pushing to lead off Jeremy Giambi, who didn't quote-unquote look like a leadoff man. Again, it was different then because of the gap between the manager's office and the GM's office. That doesn't exist now. What we did is pretty common practice now. Listen, when you don't have the money or the payroll, you do everything you can to succeed."*
> —Billy Beane

I was a little surprised the first person Michael Lewis mentioned in the acknowledgments at the end of his book was me, for "taking me to a ball game and encouraging me to pursue my line of inquiry." That was nice of him, but I've honestly got to say I do not remember that conversation other than saying, "Come on out to a ballgame and we'll talk." I remember he was around. They had told me he was writing a Sunday piece for the *New York Times*. I wasn't really concerned with it. I hadn't had a lot of relationships with the press.

Obviously, and this is mentioned a lot, the book and movie had little or no mention of the Big Three—Tim Hudson, Mark Mulder, and Barry Zito—or our two elite infielders Miguel Tejada and Eric Chavez. All those players came out of our farm system and were our key guys. They weren't the subjects of the book or movie as much as the guys Billy and Paul acquired who rounded out the roster. Plus, we spent pretty good money at the time, $9 million, on players from that season's draft, the Moneyball draft, when we had 7 of the first 39 picks but none among the top 15. The draft produced Nick Swisher, Joe Blanton, and Mark Teahan. Jeremy Brown, the hefty catcher who got on base all the time and was showcased by Lewis, played just five games in the majors, but he and others helped deepen our farm system.

"The ownership role in supporting the front office and player development department wasn't given the credit it deserved by a long shot, and Moneyball is a perfect example with the 20 wins in a row. It was all about the one signing of Scott Hatteberg. Not about the starting rotation or third baseman or shortstop. People could put their arms around the story, but it did not do justice to what was going on with all the people who helped get the players and develop them. I'll be the first to admit the wealth of new information gives you more assets to develop that talent. But it ain't just about the numbers; it's also about the human side. It's about coaching up. Otherwise, anybody can just read the percentages, and players would develop themselves."

—Tony La Russa

Chapter 23

20-Game Win Streak

MY MOTHER LOVED MIGUEL TEJADA. She insisted on me bringing her down to the clubhouse before games to see Miguel. She hugged him. He hugged her. I don't think anyone loved me owning the A's more than my mother, and a big reason was Miguel Tejada. She was very religious and appreciated that Miguel made the sign of the cross before at-bats.

Miguel had a great career and was a wonderful shortstop, and his most outstanding year for us was 2002. He was the American League's Most Valuable Player and helped us win 103 games. This was a year after Jason Giambi signed with the Yankees, and Miguel gave us two MVP winners in three years.

The most memorable part about that season was our 20-game win streak, which broke the American League record. I remember the streak vividly because so many players contributed and came up big, and it was such an exciting time for the town. It really bonded everybody. Every game, someone made the big play or got the big hit or threw the big pitch. Before the streak, we were four and a half games out of first place. After, we were three and a half up. From August 13 to September 4, we couldn't be beaten. We started the streak at home, swept a 10-game road trip, and returned to the Coliseum to break the league record, which had been held by the 1947 Yankees.

Of course, Miguel played a major role. He homered in the ninth inning to win the 18th game and the next day singled in the ninth to win the 19th, walk-off hits on consecutive days. He was such a clutch player. But up and down the roster, we had contributors. Tim Hudson and Barry Zito each won four games during the streak, and Eric Chavez hit six home runs. It wasn't just the main guys. Cory Lidle, who was a pleasant surprise for us, had four starts, gave up one earned run, and got credit for three of the wins. John Mabry hit four homers. Billy Koch, our closer, who seemed to pitch every night during the streak, saved nine games and won three more, the final three.

After Miguel got the game-winning hits in the 18th and 19th games, the 20th game featured a walk-off hit too. They made the movie about that one. That was a wild game, an exasperating game. By the third inning, we were up 11–0 over Kansas City, and the Coliseum was one big party. Then the Royals started chipping away, five runs in the fourth and another five in the eighth. They scored again in the ninth, and before you knew it, it was 11–11.

I remember how much my family enjoyed the streak, including my grandkids, but I had to break away during that last game. We had the quarterly owners' meetings in Chicago, so I had to fly out with Mike Crowley. After watching the first few innings with Sam Spear in our suite, we moved to a couple of seats near my family behind the A's dugout and eventually went down to the clubhouse to watch the final moments with Sam, who was going to drive us to the airport.

In the bottom of the ninth, with one out, Art Howe pulled Eric Byrnes for a pinch-hitter. It was Scott Hatteberg, who had been signed by Billy Beane and Paul DePodesta before the season to play first base for Giambi. That was a major theme in *Moneyball*. Hatteberg was a career catcher and able to scoop the ball because he had certain techniques as a catcher. I'm not sure he was ever a great first baseman, but when he came to bat, you felt reasonably comfortable with him. He wasn't going to hit home runs like Giambi, but he might get on base with a hit or a walk. He was fairly consistent. So when he hit for Byrnes, you had a good feeling. Everything was going right for us at that time. Sure enough, he stepped in the box and hit a home run to right field, and we won 12–11. We had our 20 wins.

Hatteberg gets the credit. He made the movie work. They had to make a hero out of somebody, and Scott was the guy with the most memorable hit in the streak. That's a home run we'll never stop seeing. It was a great experience. I couldn't believe the Royals came all the way back, but we pulled it out. It was just amazing how we kept winning day after day.

"You talk about losing momentum. Here we are in the fourth inning leading 11–0 with Hudson on the mound. I have to admit, I committed the cardinal sin. I looked over at a couple of our coaches, Rick Peterson and Ken Macha, and said, 'Don't tell me we're finally going to have a laugher.' They said, 'Don't say that.' All of a sudden, we had to get out of a jam in the ninth to keep it a tie game, setting it up for Hatteberg. Baseball, what a game."

—Art Howe

The 20th win gave us a perfect homestand, and the streak finally ended with a loss in Minnesota. The momentum carried us through the rest of the season, and we won 9 of our last 11. It didn't help us in the playoffs. We lost the first round in five games to the Twins.

Miguel played one more season in Oakland before leaving as a free agent, and my mother never stopped following him. She was in her 80s, and he was like a hero to her. It wasn't easy to go from our suite to the clubhouse. It was a good walk and a couple of elevators. But she'd always say, "We've got to say hello to Miguel." When he'd come back to town, he'd come out of the clubhouse to see her. He was never too busy. I was so impressed with that young man. In one of their visits, my mom gave him a three-decade rosary made by nuns who formed an order in Mexico. He thanked her. Miguel was a great story, a kid signed at an early age from the Dominican Republic who developed in our farm system. My mom saw him come up as a rookie and blossom. After that 2003 season, we weren't able to pay him what he was worth, and he got his big contract in Baltimore. My mom said, "You should have signed Miguel." She was right.

Chapter 24

La Russa, Howe, and Macha

BILLY BEANE AND I got in our share of arguments. I didn't care for the way he micromanaged managers. He was telling the manager what to do and how to do it. No other team was doing that 25 years ago. Billy really micromanaged Art Howe, pretty much told him what to do before games, and got involved in Ken Macha's business too. Much more than other general managers did at that time.

You can't say that style is not successful. Howe and Macha did well, and we won. It's done today, and I don't want to point fingers, but it got frustrating for me. I like to be successful; I don't like to lose. You've got to be on top of your game no matter what to keep the edge. I respected that and put the team in Sandy Alderson's hands, then Billy's, and they were working a different way with managers.

Not so much with Tony La Russa. Tony's contract was expiring in Oakland about the time I was getting there, and everyone knew what Tony meant to the franchise. Four division titles, three pennants, and a World Series title. He did a tremendous job with some great teams and great players I got to know a little, though I didn't always know how to approach these guys and didn't force it. These were legendary A's before I showed up. Rickey Henderson was on the field a lot for us and a big help teaching base running to younger guys. Dave Stewart was like an ambassador, very helpful during the transition between the Haases and us, and I appreciated everything he brought forth. He was very well-liked and had a calming demeanor. I got along well with Dennis Eckersley, who was very personable and wrote me a nice letter after we sponsored a party for him in Cooperstown for his Hall of Fame induction.

When I came to the A's, we were going to be rebuilding, and we all agreed we needed a manager who'd be good for young guys, somebody reasonably inexpensive, at least cheaper than Tony. Everybody was scared to tell Tony we couldn't pay him what he was worth, and nobody wanted to take it on with a 10-foot pole. I did it. We took a walk all around the Oakland Estuary. He was interested in staying and had reservations about going to the National League, and I said everything I could to discourage him from staying, suggesting it was going to be a while before we started winning because we were going down a different road with a lot of younger players. It wasn't going to be fun for him. He would have to play a lot of rookies. He said he could go along with that. I wasn't doing a very good job of persuading him. He wanted to come back. I finally convinced him, and he made the decision to go to St. Louis. I didn't want to chisel him down. I didn't offer him less money. I didn't think that was right.

We became friends. He liked me. I liked him. I told him he should meet my wife, and he drove all the way down to our home to meet Pat. They hit it off. It worked out well for Tony. He got the deal in St. Louis, spent 16 years with the Cardinals, and twice won the World Series. When the A's played an interleague series in St. Louis, he took me through the clubhouse and introduced me to his players, a really nice gesture. He never held a grudge against me. I have a lot of respect for Tony and have contributed to his Animal Rescue Foundation in Walnut Creek since day one, a great cause.

"I had a real attachment to the A's going back to when I signed as a player, and when the Haas family sold the team, I had a real interest and concern about what was next. I had known Ken Hofmann from our area, a philanthropist and great example for all of us who wanted to give back. As I got to know Steve, I realized he had a sincere interest in A's baseball and really wanted to go on with what the Haas family had done as far as getting the franchise back to where it was highly respected. The strength was their scouting and player development, and they didn't turn that over because they recognized the quality of what they had in the system."

—Tony La Russa

After Tony, it became possible for Sandy and Billy to use managers how they saw fit, which was the case with Howe and Macha, both good guys. I got along very well with Art and frequently visited him in his office. He was our manager for seven years, and we went from having the worst record in the majors in 1997, our second year of ownership, to three straight playoff appearances with Art in 2000, 2001, and 2002 and winning more than 100 games in both 2001 and 2002. I always liked Art and respected him as a person, and I thought he did a good job as manager, but eventually we just didn't feel he was in our plans.

We got along fine, but I didn't appreciate something Art did at the end. He went to the press as his ally, saying he wasn't getting enough money, arguing a case for a new contract, and I didn't like that. The press took his side and said we were too cheap to pay him. He was asking for a lot more money than we thought we could pay. That turned us off. Billy wasn't anxious to re-sign him; I wasn't anxious to re-sign him. After the 2002 season, Billy made a deal with Steve Phillips, the Mets' general manager, for Art to get out of his contract in Oakland and accept a four-year deal for $9.4 million in New York. No way in the world could we pay him that much, so it turned out better for Art.

"I had a year left on my contract with the A's. At that point, my relationship with Billy was not good. I remember when the 2001 season started, he insisted on playing Terrence Long in center and Johnny Damon in left, which I wasn't a big fan of. I thought to myself, 'OK, we'll go this way, let it play out a little bit.' Sure enough, Terrence didn't play well at times in center. I called Billy after a while and said, 'I'm putting Johnny in center, period.' We went off from there. Don't get me wrong. Billy did a great job as a general manager. Some of the moves he made were really outstanding. The Jermaine Dye move was off the charts. What a player. So I had a chance to go somewhere I'd get paid a lot better. I thought with the Mets, having a four-year deal, they'd give me a chance to rebuild like we did in Oakland and to an extent in Houston. The Mets lost 105 games the year before, a long way from where they wanted to be. Well, I found out quickly they were not going to be patient in New York."

—Art Howe

Macha was our bench coach under Art, and I denied the Red Sox's request to interview him to be manager in March 2002. The Red Sox wanted Macha and knew him well because he had been in their farm system, but I told them they couldn't talk with him because it was already spring training, a few weeks before the season opened, and we wanted him to eventually be our manager. Billy wanted Macha to replace Art. I asked Billy if he thought Macha would be capable, and he said yes, very much. We didn't have any other backup. If it were the wintertime, sure. But we were getting ready for the season. It would have solved the Red Sox's problem but would not have solved ours. You should not be interfering with another team unless it's the off-season. I said no. They hired Grady Little. After the season, Art left for the Mets and Macha became our manager. That's what we wanted. He was a great manager. I liked Macha but didn't know he'd be as good as he was. His first season, we got to the playoffs for the fourth straight year. Little managed two years in Boston, and then the Red Sox hired another of our coaches, Terry Francona, who won the World Series in his first year, 2004, and again in 2007.

> *"I'm not quite sure I was always considered their future manager. I'm going to call a little BS on that, regardless of whether a team wanted to hire me in spring training or whenever. I had been in Montreal when our hitting coach, Hal McRae, was hired to manage the Royals in midseason. After that 2002 season, I was interviewed at least five places. I could've easily gone to Milwaukee. I could have gone to the Cubs if Dusty Baker stayed in San Francisco. But I think Steve was a straight shooter. I loved working for Steve. He was very demanding. But you know what? I loved playing for Dick Williams. I like people who talk straight. Dick was a little harsh sometimes, but he tried to teach you the game. Steve would come around, often on Sundays, and ask the blunt questions, and he wanted straight answers. That's what I gave him. No sugarcoating from either side. He was good with you if you were honest. He valued my opinion."*
>
> —Ken Macha

Bob Geren took over for Macha after I sold the A's and managed for four and a half years, but they didn't win again until Bob Melvin started managing. Melvin's probably one of the best managers I've seen and is very level-headed, with a lot of knowledge. After the 2021 season, the A's let Melvin out of his contract to manage in San Diego and then hired Mark Kotsay, who played for the A's at the end of our ownership and had a way about him that made him likable and acceptable. I was very impressed with Kotsay. He went out of his way to talk with me, and he struck me as someone you could take a bet on. He's smart, knows the game, and is a no-nonsense guy. I like that hire. They made the right choice, in my opinion.

Chapter 25

Hudson, Mulder, and Zito

WHEN I BOUGHT THE A's, we didn't have a lot of pitching. Tim Hudson, Mark Mulder, and Barry Zito, all great draft picks by our scouting department, were a few years from emerging in the big leagues.

It was rough when I arrived. The team was coming off three straight losing seasons and, starting with 1996, would have losing records for three more years. The pitching wasn't getting it done. As a former pitcher, I was more partial to building a team around pitching than home run hitters. You've got to have both, but it starts with pitching. Luckily, big-time pitchers were on the way, with Hudson getting drafted in 1997, Mulder in 1998, and Zito in 1999. We were very fortunate to draft and develop those guys. They kept blossoming and blossoming. All starters coming out of big colleges, all homegrown pitchers who would become the Big Three, replacing Atlanta's Greg Maddux, Tom Glavine, and John Smoltz as the best trio in the game.

Now that was a treat. It was so enjoyable going to games and seeing one of those three starters dominate. The 2000 season was the first all three were on the roster together, and it's no coincidence we made the playoffs four straight years starting in 2000. We rounded out the rotation over the years with Cory Lidle, Gil Heredia, Ted Lilly, and others, but it was the Big Three we could always rely on as consistent starters who could pitch deep into games and give us opportunities to win.

These were some of my favorite players during my ownership. Naturally, I've got to side with pitchers. I truly liked Hudson, who had the heart of a lion and slyness of a fox. If you were to ask which was my favorite player during the ownership, I'd say Hudson. He wasn't big, but I always felt good about him on the mound because he gave you everything he had. Mulder was a big guy, but boy, a great athlete and outstanding competitor, a fast worker who took little time between pitches. His athleticism still shows today with how good he is on the golf course. Zito was a more crafty lefty, showing you a lot of good stuff but sneaky fast with his fastball, and once he got in a groove, he was tough to beat. I liked Zito as well.

Sometimes I'd revert to my own pitching days and wonder why they did certain things. I'd see Hudson and Mulder together and say, "Let me ask you guys, on 0–2 pitches, when you're trying to make the batter chase for strike three, why don't you throw one low and away and make them go fishing?" I'd always throw low and away on 0–2. I asked them why they didn't do that, and they said it would be easier for the catcher to miss it, and that could move up a runner. If the pitch goes high, the catcher could just reach up. My theory was that a hitter would be more tempted to swing at low and away than up high. Well, I deferred to them.

After the 2004 season, shortly before we sold the team to the Fishers, we traded Hudson to Atlanta and Mulder to St. Louis. It was a sad time in my book because I was there when they first came up. They were key parts of those teams and, obviously, in the prime of their careers when we traded them. Hudson did very well with the Braves. Mulder had just the one healthy year in St. Louis. Zito later signed with the Giants. They were all instrumental for us, along with our star hitters Jason Giambi and Miguel Tejada and all the others who filled in. I always felt we could go a lot farther with good pitching than good hitting. We ended up having both, plus a very good defense. I just think we weren't going to come up with the money to satisfy Hudson and Mulder. Their years in Oakland, we signed all the Big Three through their arbitration years, four-year extensions for all of them. It worked out well for us, and it worked out well for them. Apparently, because they never growled about it.

The Big Three. I gravitated toward watching those guys and probably was more enthralled with them than our hitters. I loved the home runs, but I saw enough of those against me. I really enjoyed watching how Hudson, Mulder, and Zito focused on their craft and succeeded in helping the team in different ways.

I kept telling myself we were lucky to have them. The fourth starter might have been a question mark, but those three always were going to carry us. Who knew they were going to be that good? Well, our guys in the system did a great job with the draft and development process, such a big difference from when I bought the team and saw the disappointing pitching in place at the time.

Chapter 26

McGwire, Giambi, and Tejada

THE A'S HAD SOME wonderful hitters during our ownership. We weren't always able to keep them around when they became free agents, but it was a joy watching them hit.

When we came in, Mark McGwire was in his prime and hitting home runs at an alarming pace, 52 in our first year, the most in the majors. One of the best years in his career. He didn't often hit for a high average, but he batted .312 that year and led the league in on-base percentage for the first time.

It was great to have Mark in the middle of our lineup, but we had a losing season and needed to rebuild our roster and farm system if we were going to turn ourselves into a winner. Sandy Alderson knew that. Everyone knew that. There was no way we could keep McGwire, who didn't want to be part of a rebuilding program. We would have loved to be able to afford to keep him, but there was no way. Mark was a great player with the A's, an All-Star many times over and a champion on one of history's great teams that played in the World Series three straight years. But the team was turning over and moving in a new direction.

Mark was becoming a free agent after the 1997 season, and we would have had to give him an enormous contract. We didn't want to go down that road and traded him to St. Louis that July for three prospects.

Mark got to play for Tony La Russa, who had moved to the Cardinals after his contract ran out in Oakland. He went on to break the homers record the following year, which might not have been a major surprise because he hit a combined 58 for us and St. Louis in 1997, three short of Roger Maris's record. But when he shot past 61 and got to 70 in that 1998 competition with Sammy Sosa, that was amazing.

The McGwire trade didn't help us turn it around. In return, we received T.J. Mathews, Eric Ludwick, and Blake Stein, all pitchers who spent very little time in Oakland. I wish we could have gotten more for McGwire. I'm still disturbed about that, but it set the stage for our next step and allowed younger guys to make names for themselves. Including Jason Giambi, who was able to move to first base, his natural position. Jason was a good guy and really got us going along with Matt Stairs, Miguel Tejada, Eric Chavez, and our great young pitching coming up. Jason was our ringleader. He was dependable. Everyone looked up to him and adopted his carefree personality, which carried us to a lot of wins. Jason was the American League's MVP in 2000 and runner-up to Ichiro Suzuki in 2001.

Jason was a free agent after that season, and we knew very well he wasn't coming back. We went through the exercise of trying to re-sign him, but we knew he was going to the Yankees. That's where his father wanted Jason to go—his hero was Mickey Mantle, and he was advising Jason the whole time. We threw some offers out there. We went along with it anyway, but it didn't really matter because we knew there was no chance to sign him. We knew we weren't getting him back. Jason wanted to be a Yankee, and the Yankees were going to get him one way or another. In New York, Jason couldn't get Mantle's No. 7, so he took 25, reasoning that 2 plus 5 adds up to 7. We also lost Johnny Damon, who had come over from Kansas City, and Jason Isringhausen, an outstanding closer, to free agency. We knew we couldn't keep them either. They were just out of our range.

Without Jason and the others, we had another huge year in 2002 and won 103 games, the so-called Moneyball year. We still had a lot of great players, especially in our rotation with the Hudson-Mulder-Zito trifecta. You've got to give credit where credit is due. We filled in with the right players, and all of them came through. Tejada stepped up and won the MVP in 2002, and Zito won the Cy Young Award. Miguel was eligible for free agency after the 2003 season, and here we went again. We took a different approach this time and said in spring training we weren't going to go through the exercise of negotiating and offering a deal because we knew we weren't going to pay Miguel what he could get on the open market. I took a lot of heat for that. We would have loved to have kept Miguel, but we couldn't get to the number he would have wanted. That's why we didn't pursue Miguel. Plus, I was told we had a replacement, Bobby Crosby, who came up at the end of 2003 and was the league's rookie of the year in 2004, but it would have been tough for anyone to replace Miguel, who signed in Baltimore and kept putting up big years.

"I wish I would've stayed in Oakland, but I realize it's a business. The time I was playing for Mr. Schott and all the people in Oakland was an enjoyable time. I have only good memories. I feel like I was born in Oakland and grew up there. I'm never going to forget that. I'm part of the family of the Oakland A's. We were all young and hungry to play baseball and happy to be in the big leagues. The money we were making, we were happy. We were a low-revenue team, and we won anyway."

—Miguel Tejada

Chavez was the next big hitter coming up on free agency. He had a great glove at third base and a nice bat. We took yet another approach with Chavez and signed him in spring training in 2004. We didn't want to let everybody get away. I listened to the case to bring him back, and we signed him to the biggest contract in A's history. It still is. Six years and $66 million. The press asked me how I felt after we signed him, and I said I'd let them know in five or six years. Well, we wound up selling the team in 2005. All these years later, it's still the largest contract the A's ever gave a player. Isn't that amazing? And they said *I* was a cheapskate.

We didn't think there was any way we could get close to what Tejada would get. Tejada came up earlier than Chavez and got to free agency quicker, and he was going to be a prime target for teams. I don't think his agent even bothered to talk to us about a long-term contract. When Chavez came up, I felt compelled that we had to do something after all those guys got away, so we worked it out with Chavez. At least I didn't go down in history as a guy who never signed anyone to a big contract. The Fishers haven't done that and received all that revenue sharing that we didn't receive.

"Everyone brings up the Chavez contract, which still is the biggest as far as total dollars, but another one that isn't talked about is Jermaine Dye's, three years and $32 million, coming after he broke his leg in the playoffs. It was market value, the biggest contract the team had given at that time. With Giambi, the club made a competitive offer, more than $100 million. There was a press release written. It broke down, but they were close. After that, it came down to Tejada or Chavez. They weren't going to pay for both. They chose Chavez, and that didn't work out because Tejada was the better player for longer.

"Despite the reputation the A's had for letting all their star players go to free agency, it wasn't necessarily the case except

for Tejada. Giambi chose to leave even though the A's offered him a big deal, and Billy traded Hudson and Mulder, two trades that weren't as money-driven as people think. With their ill-fated experience of bringing guys back after the 1992 season, Billy followed the Bill Walsh plan: get rid of a guy a year too early rather than a year too late. I think that played into those deals, and even after trading Mulder and Hudson, the A's contended in '05 and won the AL West in '06, so they were a contender far more than the four playoff years, actually from '99 to '06. A solid run."

—David Feldman, A's historian

A hitter I really liked was Matt Stairs, who came out of nowhere to succeed in the majors. He had power and hit lots of home runs, 38 one year, and was inexpensive because he had very little service time. He wasn't known for his defense but played right field pretty well, had a pretty good arm, and got a lot of key homers. He was a big part of the A's becoming a winner in the late 1990s. We signed him shortly after we bought the team and gave him a chance he didn't get anywhere else. That was a big thing in Oakland, giving guys opportunities. Sometimes it's about the break you get. Then bingo, you're on your way.

Stairs was a character, a good guy, fun to be around, a good ol' boy. I was drawn to him, maybe because he was from Canada and I had so many Canadian friends. When the A's were in Toronto, after a game I introduced him to Gary Kirk, my friend who helped me get on the summer baseball team in Alberta when I was in college. One time in spring training, we threw a party at my house in Palm Springs for friends from the Vintage Club and invited players. Ken Hofmann was a big part of it and asked if I'd host. He lived a block from me. I said OK. So I flew to Arizona on my plane and picked up some players and flew back to the desert. One thing I'll never forget about that flight:

We ran out of beer. It was unbelievable. Stairs and those guys had a good time.

We had a lot of wonderful hitters over the years. A couple who stood out were second basemen Mark Ellis and Marco Scutaro. Mark should have won some Gold Gloves, and Marco was a phenomenal hitter in the clutch, steady and dependable. It took him a while to get noticed. The Giants later picked him up, and he helped them win a World Series in 2012. I was happy for him.

Chapter 27

Bittersweet Octobers

WHEN WE BUILT UP THE A's, our goal every year was not just to contend but to get deep into the playoffs. Though we made the postseason four straight years, it's tough to look back. We were disappointed every year because of a combination of flukes, mental mistakes, and Derek Jeter.

Jeter took a game from us and, it turned out, the whole 2001 playoff series, thanks to his legendary flip in Game 3 that caught Jason Giambi's brother at the plate. I still can't believe Jeremy didn't slide. It was an unfortunate situation. But no excuse. Jeter came all the way from shortstop to the first-base line to take the cut from right field—the throw missed two other cutoff men—and flip the ball to the plate for the out. That's why Jeter's a Hall of Famer. People said he was out of position. Jeter's comment was that's where he was supposed to be.

We were one of the majors' best teams in the early 2000s with the four playoff appearances. But each year, we got eliminated in the opening round, and each best-of-five series went the full five games. It's like we were jinxed. Some of those playoff losses were avoidable. We blew them ourselves starting with the Yankees, the team we met in the playoffs in both 2000 and 2001. Then Minnesota. Then Boston.

It was one thing after another, always disheartening. It didn't sit well with me. We won the first two games against both the Yankees and Red Sox and led the Twins two games to one. It was hard to rationalize how good you might be. We were often the underdog and always had tough competition in the playoffs. These were great teams we faced. We caught the Yankees at the height of their dynasty. The Red Sox were on the rebound, and the year after we got them in the playoffs, they won their first World Series since 1918. The Twins were dominating their division in those years.

Though we never got past the first round, I always was proud of the team for how the players performed, how they always seemed to come on strong in the second half and how they carried good momentum into the postseason. The players always went that extra mile, and that's important to point out. We had some tremendous playoff moments, and I thank our players for how hard they worked and how well they performed.

But it's impossible to forget some of the key plays that were costly. We could have swept Boston in three games. We had a chance for a big sixth inning in Game 3 at Fenway Park, but two base-running mistakes killed us and we lost 3–1 in 11 innings. First, Eric Byrnes should have scored on a roller to the left side. He was blocked at the plate by Jason Varitek and didn't make an effort to step on the plate even with the pitcher making a bad throw and the ball rolling all the way to the backstop. Varitek came back to tag him out. A few moments later, Miguel Tejada came around third base and stopped running between third and home because he was saying Bill Mueller, the third baseman, interfered with him. He was tagged out by Varitek too. Clearly those are mental mistakes. You've got to keep running. You've got to finish the play. Get to the plate. We gave that game away. The Red Sox scored their first run early, thanks to three errors in one inning, and then came our base-running blunders. Instead of sweeping, we lost in five again. We led Game 4 by a couple of runs in the late innings but lost by a run, and we left the bases loaded in the ninth inning of the final game and again lost by a run.

> *"All these things just happened. I don't know why they always happened against us, especially with that play at third base with me. I stopped because I thought the umpire would call interference. I didn't know that rule. I should've been running. Look what happened. Those were tough losses. We were always pushing hard, working hard, and never passed the first round, but I really enjoyed getting that opportunity every year."*
>
> —Miguel Tejada

Listen, I've always been a baseball fan. You bet. To this day I'm still pulling for these A's teams all the way to the end. We had seats right there in the front row, and I loved being close to the action, but I couldn't always sit there because I'd get so frustrated when we'd lose, even in the regular season. I couldn't sit there and bite my lip and be unemotional. I'd go up to the owners' box where nobody could see me—sometimes no one was up there except my family—and I could yell and scream and do things without making a scene.

Some mistakes really bugged me. Like Giambi not sliding. And Tejada and Byrnes. Those were big games. But sometimes you'd forget how hard this game is. You'd forget they were human beings, and we all make errors. That's part of being a fan, expecting so much out of your guys. I knew the game pretty doggone well. I wouldn't say I knew all the intricacies, but I knew about the game and enjoyed talking with Art Howe quite a lot about his decision-making and thought process.

After we got eliminated by the Twins, we had a staff meeting the next day. I wanted to go down to the clubhouse to find out what was going on. Mark Ellis hit a three-run homer in the final inning of the last game, but we gave up three in the top of the ninth and lost another one-run game.

I was upset. Everyone was. We were favored to win that series. I expressed my thoughts. I wanted to talk about why we kept losing the big game. "Why can't we win the big one? It's in our grasp, and we fumble it." The subject was raw for Billy, and he exploded. He said, "I'm not going to have you rip my team. Don't come down here and run anyone down." I wasn't running anyone down. It might have been the way I came across, my tone of voice. I was just trying to figure out what was the cause of our losses. This wasn't the first time. We were all pissed.

> *"Steve left a message to come down to the clubhouse the next day. He wanted Art and all those guys there, and he kind of laid into the staff. I was steaming. It was BS. I was stewing, I'd had enough. In fairness to Steve, he backed off after I said my piece. He was just like everyone else. He was frustrated, and it carried over to the next day. Listen, in this game and business, emotions run high. We had lost some of our best players and won one more game in 2002 than we did the previous year. Everyone knew it was tough to lose to Minnesota."*
>
> **—Billy Beane**

I never got to first base in the conversation because Billy got on my case. It was going nowhere, so I figured I'd excuse myself and we'd talk later. I got up and left. After the season, we replaced Art Howe with Ken Macha.

> *"Steve was really frustrated after that Minnesota series, but I could understand it. Billy told him to lay off his staff. We were all frustrated. We felt we had the better team. We just didn't win*

the series. It's frustrating when it happens. Back-to-back years, we lost to the Yankees in the first round, and now Minnesota. You always want to get better each year, and knocking off the Twins would've been good for us, but we ran into a team that got hot at the right time. That was David Ortiz's introduction to the postseason, and he became one of the best October hitters ever. Tim Hudson had a bad hip but wanted to go out and pitch for us. We probably shouldn't have pitched him. He pitched the first and fourth games, and we lost them both. He felt he could pitch without hurting the team, but it became obvious he wasn't himself. I can sleep with that because he was our guy. You've got to love Huddy. We lost the final game, and I can understand Steve's frustration. Everybody had his heart set on beating the Twins."

—Art Howe

"Billy did protect us. Mr. Schott was in his feelings. That's OK. You've got to allow people to be in their feelings. He had a right to be in his feelings. Nothing we could do about it. Minnesota beat us. I didn't take it personal. I don't think the other guys took it personal, but Billy did what a general manager was supposed to do: defend his team. Even though it was the owner. Billy's been doing this a long gosh-darn time. He knows when to fire a bullet and when to keep his distance. He was disappointed too. Yeah, we should've beaten the Twins."

—Ron Washington, former A's coach

Did I think we'd ever get to the World Series? That would have been a dream, something extraordinary. Everything would have had to be aligned perfectly for us. We kept losing big-time players but kept replacing them with players who did a great job. We won as much as any other team in the regular season. A break here or there in October could have taken us deeper, but the postseason is a crapshoot. The ball has to bounce the right way. It can come down to one pitch, one at-bat, one base-running play. If it weren't for Jeter's unbelievable play, we could have gone on to the next round. Unfortunately, things happened you won't see again in 50 years.

But I must say, credit needs to be given to a lot of people who made us as good as we were in those years: the players, coaches, front office, scouts, and fans who showed up in droves during the playoffs. For the money, the A's were the best ticket in town for spectators. We'd top 50,000 for some of those games, and the Coliseum was electric. It's too bad we couldn't get past that first round, and I'm sorry we didn't bring another World Series to Oakland.

Chapter 28

Radio, TV, and Tommy Lasorda

I GREW UP LISTENING TO BASEBALL on the radio. We didn't have the major leagues in the Bay Area when I was a kid, but we had the Pacific Coast League, and I can still remember Jack Macdonald and Don Klein broadcasting the San Francisco Seals; many of those games they recreated through Western Union transmissions. I'd turn on the radio in bed at night when I was supposed to be sleeping to listen to the Seals games. The broadcasts were wonderful. Macdonald was very colorful and called himself the Old Walnut Farmer and said home runs went through "Aunt Maggie's window," and Klein later called 49ers and Stanford games.

I still listen to radio broadcasts, which are so important to the sport's fabric and marketing. I listen to A's games as much as I can. I enjoy their broadcast team. On the TV side too. I remember suggesting Glen Kuiper and bringing him in. He's still calling games and doing a very good job. Dallas Braden joined the broadcast team a few years ago as a color guy and is a good fit with Glen's style.

I really liked Ray Fosse, a former catcher who played for the A's championship teams in the 1970s. Unfortunately, Ray stepped away from the booth during the 2021 season to battle cancer, and we lost him shortly after the season. I had a special bond with Ray and his family, and his daughters were nice enough to invite me to their weddings. Ray was always on your side, which meant so much to everyone with the A's and their fans. The baseball world misses Ray. He was really a solid guy.

The broadcaster I loved the most was Bill King. He was my favorite, a hero to me. I liked him personally too, and he came over to me quite a bit to talk. We got along well. I heard him call games in so many sports, and he was great in all of them. He was the voice of Oakland. Warriors, Raiders, A's. So versatile. You just couldn't believe how good he was. I loved his Raiders calls. That's when I first got hooked. "Holy Toledo," his signature call, will always be remembered in the Bay Area. What an announcer. I'm glad I got to know him.

"I was very lucky. I did not have a lot of experience at that point. They took a chance. Hey, I'm still here. I guess it turned out well. They didn't have to do that, and they did. For the rest of my life, I'll always be just incredibly grateful for Steve and others responsible for me calling A's games, including Mike Crowley, Ken Pries, Tom Raponi, and Ted Griggs. Right place, right time. I remember it like it was yesterday. I had just gotten married, and we were going to get a Christmas tree. Ken Pries called and said, 'We've got an offer for you.' I had to pull over. I'm sure Mr. Schott had a lot to do with it because he was the owner. The fact he likes my work means a lot to me."

—Glen Kuiper

When we bought the team, Bill and Lon Simmons were the radio crew. They're both in baseball's Hall of Fame as Ford C. Frick Award winners. Lon had mentioned that he'd like to scale back a bit and maybe call just home games in the 1996 season. He didn't need to be full time, and he preferred to know his status sooner rather than later so he could consider other things. I had Ed Alvarez, who was handling these things at the time, ask Lon if we could work out a shorter schedule for him, maybe take some games off and have someone else come in for us to try out, see what he could offer.

It was never my intention to fire Lon Simmons. It was my intention for somebody to sit down with Lon and ask if he'd want to pull back on his time. I never told Ed we were going to terminate Lon, but Ed left a voice mail essentially telling him we were going in a different direction, that we were not going to use him the next year. I had known Ed since college, and I was surprised it happened. I had no knowledge of that. I wouldn't have told somebody like Lon anything like this over the phone instead of face-to-face. I enjoyed listening to Lon from when he and Russ Hodges, another Hall of Fame broadcaster, called Giants games, and Lon was the voice of the 49ers as well. It came out publicly that we fired him, and I took the hit.

If I had it to do over again, and I've said this, I would have hired Sam Spear right away and used him in many ways. In this case, I would have talked to Sam to see how to handle the situation. It was unfortunate how it happened. The following season, Lon returned to the Giants, with whom he had broadcast when they moved west in 1958, and worked part time for several more years. Ken Korach replaced Lon in the A's booth and joined Bill King, and that worked out great. Korach is very good and still calling games on radio today with Vince Cotroneo. The thing is, we weren't able to capitalize much on TV and radio revenue, which cut into the amount of money we could spend.

"The A's had the highest payroll in 1991, and it's cool to say that, but it wasn't much higher than the 10th-highest payroll. Now, the

difference between 1st and 10th is $100 million. Payroll disparity took off after the Yankees got their 12-year, $500 million TV deal with MSG Network, basically an extra $41 million a year starting in 1991. Teams started lining up for huge regional TV deals, but there's still a discrepancy now. Look at the American League West. The Angels have a $3 billion deal, $138 million a year in local TV rights, plus 25 percent ownership stake, while the A's get $48 million with zero ownership. The A's started dealing with this disparity in the Schott-Hofmann years. By then, it was no longer a level playing field."

—David Feldman, A's historian

Games weren't televised when I was a kid. They didn't begin showing the World Series to the West Coast until the 1950s. The first televised World Series game that stuck out for me was in 1956: Yankees-Dodgers, and Vin Scully and Mel Allen were on the call. I was a freshman in college, and Don Larsen threw a perfect game. I'll never forget that. After the final pitch, Yogi Berra jumped into Larsen's arms. I was never a big Yankees fan, but you've got to respect what he accomplished on that stage. The Yankees had such great pitchers when I was a kid. Allie Reynolds, Eddie Lopat, Vic Raschi, Whitey Ford. Don Larsen wasn't a Hall of Famer, but he had an extraordinary moment in the World Series.

I had a pretty cool experience with Don Larsen. He pitched for the Giants after they moved to San Francisco and faced the Yankees in the 1962 World Series. He later worked for a paper company in San Jose and sometimes would pitch in our local semipro games. He was asked to come over, hang out, and play a little ball at night. I thought it was great being in the same dugout with him. He was just a regular guy, but I was too intimidated to talk with him.

I couldn't help but think of Don Larsen during the 2020 World Series when Tampa Bay's Blake Snell had given up two hits and was leading Game 6 when he was pulled by his manager, Kevin Cash. The Rays lost the game, giving the Dodgers the series. This guy Snell was amazing. He did an outstanding job and was taken out after 73 pitches. Imagine that. You've got to have a feel for your pitcher. It's his last game of the year. Keep him in. If you have him throw 100 pitches, big deal, right? Years ago, they never would have considered taking him out. Anyway, the Dodgers finally won the World Series, their first since beating the A's in 1988. I've never been a Dodgers fan, but after all those years, they deserved it.

Speaking of the Dodgers, there was no greater ambassador in the game than Tommy Lasorda, and I was sitting in the crowd with him in Anaheim during Game 2 of the 2002 World Series. We're shooting the breeze, and Tommy says, "I'm hungry. I better eat something. I need a hot dog." So he grabs a foot-long and one of those tiny mustard packets and squirts it all over the back of Bill Bartholomew of the Braves. Tommy says, "Don't worry about it," then he grabs a napkin and smears the mustard all over what looked like a thousand-dollar sportscoat, just making it worse. I'm not sure Bartholomew realized what was going on. It was a riot. When I got up to go to the restroom, it took 20 minutes because of a long line. Then Tommy got up to go to the restroom and returned in just a few minutes. He said once he got there, the whole place parted. They let him walk to the front of the line right up to the trough. That was Tommy.

I was in Las Vegas when I came across an avid Lasorda fan, an avid Dodgers fan. I went down to the hotel lobby early in the morning to get a bite to eat and cup of coffee, and this young guy in his early 30s was ranting and raving and making all kinds of hell, mouthing off like I couldn't believe, and telling the front desk he was suing the hotel. He was getting louder and louder and saying the hotel discriminated against him and took advantage of him because he was Hispanic. Turns out, he had been locked out of his room earlier in the morning, and embarrassed, he had to come down in his boxers. I told him I'd be embarrassed too. We got to talking, and it came out that he grew up around Chavez Ravine and loved the Dodgers and that I owned the A's. I told him the Lasorda stories from the '02 Series and had him eating out of my hand. He calmed down and was the nicest guy in the world. He knew all about the A's and Moneyball and how "Derek Jeter stole that playoff game from you." I tried to turn it around and smooth it over. Now he forgot what he was mad about. He asked for my autograph, and I said I'd send him a copy of my book.

Chapter 29

Yankees Stories

EVERYONE KNOWS YOGI BERRA has said a lot of strange things—Yogi-isms, as they're known. He once told me, "You know, I don't even remember saying half those things." People might know another way he might have put it: "I never said half the things I said."

I was lucky to get to know Yogi on a personal level. We became friends when I owned the A's. George Graziadio, who cofounded Imperial Bank, introduced me to Yogi, and we played a lot of golf together, including in Palm Springs—he hit 'em left-handed like he did in baseball—and our wives got to know each other. Yogi often played in the Bob Hope Desert Classic, and I was fortunate to play in the pro-am a few times. George would invite Yogi to dinner, and I got to know him pretty well.

A few years after he opened the Yogi Berra Museum and Learning Center in New Jersey, I was in New York for an A's-Yankees playoff series, and he invited Pat and me to see the museum. I told him we couldn't make it because it was closed Mondays and we were going back to California, so he offered to open it Monday and give us a personal tour. It was fantastic, and I'm glad I've been able to contribute financially to the museum. He was so proud of it. What I remember more than anything is all the autographed balls by Yankees, so many of the guys who played with him.

One name popped out, a guy who was an All-American at Santa Clara: Bill Renna. He also played football in college and got drafted by the Rams. Bill's first year in the big leagues, he played with Yogi on the 1953 Yankees, a team that went on to beat the Brooklyn Dodgers in the World Series. Bill later played for the A's and Red Sox as Ted Williams's teammate, almost like a fourth outfielder. Bill was a local hero. He was 15 years older, but I got to know him very well. He told me how it was when you'd get hurt back then. You played hurt or you lost your job. He said one time he broke a toe and couldn't wear a shoe, so he cut off the end of his shoe and painted his white sanitary sock black because he didn't want anyone to know he had broken his toe, because he might not have gotten his job back. He couldn't have been nicer. He went to work for a company that sold cement, Pacific Ready Mix, and we bought tons for our building foundations. I got to know him from that standpoint too—a great guy. When he died, I spoke at his wake and mentioned it was a big thrill to see his signed ball in Yogi's museum.

I remember one night we were out to dinner with Yogi, and Pat asked him, "Why don't you make up with George Steinbrenner?" They had that feud that lasted nearly 15 years, going back to George firing Yogi as manager early in the 1985 season and Yogi vowing never to return to Yankee Stadium as long as George ran the team. When Pat asked Yogi the question, Yogi's wife, Carmen, chimed in and said, "Well, I'll tell you why. Yogi's got a hard head, a harder head than George's." Shortly thereafter, during the 1999 season, they did make up and got to be buddies again.

I'm glad they did because Yogi belonged at Yankee Stadium. I enjoyed his company and have great memories of him. He loved to talk about his childhood as a neighbor of Joe Garagiola in St. Louis. They were so poor they had to improvise for a ball and bat to play in the streets, and they remained the best of friends.

> *"Yogi seemed to like to talk to me, I guess because we are both Italian. I remember Carmen said she asked him to clean the attic of all the 'junk,' and all that 'junk' happened to be all the trophies, World Series rings, bats, balls, etc. Well, Yogi had enough of that 'junk' that he built his own museum in New Jersey. When he took us on the tour, it was amazing. He was having a fundraiser to build a patio and was selling bricks, so we bought one in the name of each of our grandchildren. Both Carmen and Yogi were very interesting and open people. I remember asking Yogi when he knew it was time to retire, and he said, 'When I struck out three times in one game, that's when I retired.' I must say, Steve and I did so many interesting things because of baseball. So many doors were opened that two little kids from San Jose would never have experienced. I thank God and Steve for a most fascinating life."*
>
> —Pat Schott

One time at Yankee Stadium, we arrived early and were sitting with George when Yogi walked in. Knowing we were friends, George would ask Yogi to sit in his box and then put up yellow tape you see for crime scenes to reserve seats for Pat and me and Yogi and Carmen. Anyway, someone had given Yogi a drink, and he set it down in front of the first row of seats on a little ledge. Well, he accidentally hit the drink with his hand and knocked it over the ledge and down on the people below. They looked up and screamed, "You SOBs," and one guy raised a fist. Pat said, "If those people it spilled on knew it was Yogi's, they would have loved it." That's how much they adored Yogi in New York.

Another time George and I were sitting together in his suite at Yankee Stadium, Tim Hudson was throwing a no-hitter. Neither George nor I said a word about it, but I knew what was going on. Midgame, George said, "I don't know if you're following that closely, but your pitcher is on the verge of a no-hitter." Jinxed him. Right after that, one of the Yankees got a base hit. I remember that as well as anything. Thanks, George.

"Compare George and Steve? George was the total opposite. Totally bombastic. Steve never fired me. George fired me two or three times, but I always got my job back. I was always told by Al Rosen or Cedric Tallis or whoever the GM was, 'He'll blow off steam, Mickey. Come back tomorrow, you'll be all right, he'll forget about it.' So the next day, it was, 'Where's Morabito? Get him in here.' 'Well, you friggin' fired me last night.' No, Steve never fired me."
—Mickey Morabito, A's traveling secretary,
who had a similar role with the Yankees

I got to know one of the greatest of all Yankees who happened to be one of the greatest of all A's: Reggie Jackson. When I took over the team, I realized Reggie's number had never been retired in Oakland, which I thought was a shame. So we retired No. 9 in 2004. Here's a guy who was a main force on three World Series championship teams. We already had Catfish Hunter's and Rollie Fingers's numbers retired. There were stories that Reggie had a falling out with the team. Stories that he wanted to get paid to have his number retired. I didn't know about any of that. We reached out to Reggie. It's something that should have been done much earlier. He was receptive. He didn't ask for anything. He just said, "Let's make a donation to the Oakland schools." He was concerned about the schools. That was right in my wheelhouse. With help from corporations, a donation on Reggie's behalf was made to the schools for $150,000, and I wrote a check for another $25,000.

Finally, 11 years after he was inducted into the Hall of Fame, we had Reggie Jackson Day at the Coliseum and retired Reggie's No. 9. He now had his numbers retired by two teams—he was No. 44 with the Yankees. Reggie still was working for George, who hired him in 1993 as a special adviser, but it was nice that the A's were able to honor Reggie for all he did for the organization.

Part Five

SELLING THE A's

Chapter 30

Territorial Rights?
No Such Thing!

THE 49ERS MOVED FROM CANDLESTICK PARK to Santa Clara in 2014, right where I wanted to build a new ballpark for the A's.

We were in discussions to relocate the team from the East Bay to the South Bay, a very good location in the heart of Silicon Valley next to Great America amusement park. The plan was for a baseball-only facility, much smaller than the Coliseum, that would attract a lot of fans and corporate sponsorships. I knew the city-owned land well enough to know the A's would flourish there. I was in talks with the Santa Clara City Council, which was on board. At the time, Santa Clara was far more serious than San Jose, which wanted to be in the hunt but wasn't far along in the process. Santa Clara, on the other hand, was well prepared and brought about 20 people to my office, including the mayor and city council members, to show their interest. They wanted us in the worst way before there was any talk of the 49ers, and I had connections down there. The idea was a good one, especially because the Coliseum no longer was feasible for baseball after the

Raiders returned and reconstructed the place. The Santa Clara site was 45 minutes from from the Coliseum, and it would have been perfect down there.

There was one problem, and it's a reason the A's still play at the Coliseum, and a reason we sold the team to the Fishers in 2005: territorial rights. Or at least perceived territorial rights. There weren't really any territorial rights. Strictly arbitrary on the part of Bud Selig, the commissioner who claimed the Giants had the rights to the South Bay, but nothing gave the Giants full rights to the South Bay. It should have been wide open. It really wasn't anybody's territory. In fact, the whole thing stemmed from ballpark elections the Giants had before I bought the A's.

This was a time when the Giants were more likely to relocate than the A's. Bob Lurie wanted out of Candlestick Park and tried four times in elections to secure funding for a ballpark—two in San Francisco, one in San Jose, and one in Santa Clara. I got involved in the Santa Clara one. Lurie went to the Haas family to talk about getting the measure on the ballot in San Jose and Santa Clara, and the Haas family said OK. They didn't care. When Lurie got voted down four times, he put the team up for sale and made a deal to sell to a Florida group that would move the team to St. Petersburg. The National League owners didn't let it happen and provided an opportunity for San Francisco businesspeople to step up, and that's when Peter Magowan's group bought the Giants in December 1992, three years before we purchased the A's. Both teams had new ownerships that weren't involved in the initial talk of territorial rights.

"We shared the territorial rights up to that point, the Giants and the A's. They asked if we would cede those rights to them so they could go through the referendum, and we felt that was fine....

Once the referendums failed, one could say, 'Well, maybe you should have gone back to a shared situation.' We didn't ask for it. We weren't looking to build a new stadium. That's just the way it stood."

—Wally Haas,
former A's CEO and son of former owner Walter Haas

Well, when we started looking at Santa Clara, somehow the Giants claimed they had rights to the area, and Selig backed them up. Magowan totally had Bud on his side and argued that if we moved down there, we'd have killed the Giants' market. It would have cut into their market to some degree, but by then the Giants had moved from Candlestick to their downtown site, and they would have had the whole East Bay market. That's the tradeoff. If we had moved, the Giants would have been eight miles farther away from us than they are now and drawn more fans in Oakland with us in the South Bay.

Technically, we could have gotten the green light for Santa Clara with 75 percent approval from baseball's owners. That would have superseded any so-called territorial rights, but Selig never let it get to a vote. He put the kibosh on it. If there was a vote, I would have had to do a lot of lobbying. I wasn't that strong with a lot of owners, but I knew owners wanted the A's in a healthier environment than the Coliseum. It was no different from other areas across the nation that have two baseball teams and share their markets, like New York. I could never get Selig to move at all in our direction. He was closed-minded about the situation.

"The territorial thing, I think the Coliseum was a bad stadium to start with, and when football came back, it was worse. Walter Haas, when he owned the team, was very generous ceding Santa Clara County to the Giants so they could build a stadium.

But when they never built it, for whatever reason, they did not include a provision that it would be revoked. I felt Oakland was mistreated by the Giants. The territory should've gone back to the A's. I disagree with Bud's decision, and I disagree with Rob Manfred. The A's should be allowed to go to Santa Clara."

—Jerry Reinsdorf, Chicago White Sox owner

"That's a screw job, to be honest. They shouldn't be the Giants' rights. That was a temporary thing. They wound up keeping it. Of course, the Giants would fight like hell before giving it up, and I understand why they would, and you're probably not going to get it back."

—Joe Lacob, Golden State Warriors owner

The Giants said it would have been no problem if we had moved somewhere else in the East Bay, but we didn't want to do that. Santa Clara made sense. We thought the best place for the A's in the East Bay was the Coliseum site.

There was never any realistic intention to move the A's outside the Bay Area. If I had gotten the word, I would have moved to Santa Clara in a heartbeat. The A's would be there now if we had gotten the green light. They'd be in a great position, two teams in the Bay Area with nice ballparks. That's no longer an option because Santa Clara is home of the 49ers.

"What you say to clubs when new owners come in is, 'This is your territory as it exists today.' So the Giants knew what their territory was, and the Oakland club knew their territory. I'm very sensitive about the territories because if you start tampering with them, where do you stop?"

—Bud Selig

Chapter 31

The Co-Owner

I OWNED THE A's FOR A DECADE and never really saw eye to eye with Ken Hofmann, my fellow owner, so the ownership wasn't destined to last forever. That's the danger when you don't form your own ownership group. In this case, officials in Oakland and Alameda County recruited us, and Ken was a bit of a loose cannon. A nice guy but a loose cannon.

You couldn't find anyone more generous and charitable. He helped underprivileged kids and gave to schools, including St. Mary's College and De La Salle High School, a football powerhouse. He was very helpful in a lot of ways to a lot of people with his charity work. We knew each other a little bit when we were handpicked to buy the A's. He was a developer from the East Bay, and I was a developer in the South Bay. He had a charity golf tournament I played in, and we had been on the same promotional trips that General Electric hosted. I found him to be a nice guy, but getting into business together can be a different story.

Long Schott

"Steve Schott and Ken Hofmann were consummate business-people, as were Walter Haas and Roy Eisenhardt, who structured the A's as a community asset. A lot of what we did was community driven, to keep the team in Oakland. I might've been a little biased toward the Haases; they could have sold the team for far more out of the market. When the team was sold, and you're Steve and Ken, who were in the real estate and homebuilding business, you'll cut the best deal you can. The thought was, as long as there was somebody local and respected, it was like, 'OK, the team's staying.'"

—Andy Dolich, former A's marketing director

I was the managing partner, but Hofmann didn't always acknowledge that, making it very difficult. Ken wouldn't buy if I wouldn't buy. He wouldn't sell if I wouldn't sell, so there was never going to be another partner. We were 50-50 financially, and even though I was the managing partner, he sometimes wanted to run the show despite the fact that Major League Baseball didn't want him to run the show. Bud Selig had to write a letter to his attorney to say he couldn't come to the owners' meetings. He'd bring his attorney to meetings and want to trump me. I don't know how many times he'd say he's in on something then say he's not in.

"Ken was very strong-willed. It could be frustrating sometimes to work for him and not know what was expected. He'd change day to day, week to week. I had to be on my toes. 'Is he going to change his mind tomorrow?' He was a very reactive person, really hard to work for. Steve was really easy to work for. You never had to worry about his direction. When you put those styles together, it's a little bit of oil and water."

—Nick Rossi, attorney for the A's and Ken Hofmann

Early in our ownership when it was clear the Raiders' return was going to have a negative effect on the A's, we met with the mayor, Elihu Harris. I had known that I would need to leave early because of another engagement set up before this meeting was called, and I assumed I left it in good hands. Well, after I left, Harris offered us $1 million to settle any complaint we might have. It was a peace offering to resolve the problems we were facing. We had to open our first season in Las Vegas because the Coliseum was under construction for the Raiders' renovation. So Harris offered $1 million in damages.

Well, Hofmann rejected it. He said forget the million bucks. He said we had bigger fish to fry. He never talked with me about it. He gave a million dollars away. That's the kind of guy he was—making rash decisions. Kind of a bulldozer approach with his decisions and comments. I thought it was a pretty good offer. He thought it was chicken feed, a drop in the bucket. I guess I never should have left the meeting, but I never anticipated any of that. We didn't just not get $1 million; we didn't get a dime. I didn't pursue it. I was more intent on trying to get the team going and trying to do well with the baseball side. Hofmann kind of closed the door on our talks with the mayor, and I didn't want to litigate at that point when I was trying to put the team in a good position to play and win while trying to get butts in the seats.

Chapter 32

Joe Lacob's Interest in the A's

JOE LACOB BOUGHT THE GOLDEN STATE WARRIORS in July 2010 and built a dynasty with Stephen Curry, Klay Thompson, Draymond Green, and Kevin Durant. The Warriors became the most dominant team in the NBA and super fun to watch.

But several years before Lacob took over the Warriors, he expressed interest in buying the A's. That kind of came out of the blue. When you own a baseball team, you receive a lot of inquiries from people asking if you're interested in selling, and our business model made it appealing to a lot of people. Lacob spoke with my attorney, Frank Nicoletti. We told him, "Here's the deal right here. If you want it, you can have it for this number. Meet the price, and it's yours." We heard he could get approved by Major League Baseball without any problem.

"This never really came out, but I had an agreement to buy the Oakland A's, literally. I'll never forget it. What happened was, even though I had a verbal agreement, as I understand it, Bud Selig, the commissioner at the time and a fraternity brother [at the University of Wisconsin] of Lew Wolff, basically did not

approve of Schott and Hofmann selling the team to someone he didn't know or wanted to control. He wouldn't approve it, and so as I understand it, he made them sell the team to Lew Wolff, who basically took my term sheet that I had negotiated and went to try to raise money, and that's how John Fisher got in on the deal. He recruited John to be the financial partner while Wolff kind of ran it. That's the story. So I had the Oakland A's agreed to with Schott and Hofmann, and it got yanked from under me. I was really pissed at Bud Selig. I easily qualified; that wasn't the issue. Bud basically did what he wanted to do, and he didn't know me.

"So I learned a little lesson from that, which is it's not all about money. You've got to have the right friends in these leagues. Not even the seller can control it sometimes. It's why I then went and, at the advice of [then–NBA commissioner] David Stern, became a minority limited partner in the Boston Celtics, a team I had a minority interest in for five years. I got to know David and everyone in the league and other owners. When the Warriors came up in 2010, I had an advantage, ironically—maybe my only advantage—over Larry Ellison, which was I knew everybody in the league really well. It's interesting. The reaction to what happened with the A's kind of helped me get the Warriors."

—Joe Lacob

There had been someone else trying to buy the team, Jonathan Ledecky, who was close to Bud Selig and had tried to purchase other teams. If Bud gives you a name, you've got to follow through. You know what I'm saying? But Ledecky couldn't qualify because he had a lot of his money in the stock market. Two or three guys were referred to us by Bud, but issues came up or they were not able to secure the financing.

Lacob came later, and this was before the Bay Area knew him as the Warriors' owner. He did very well with the Warriors and got a beautiful new venue in San Francisco, not to mention three championships. Who knows what would have happened had he bought the A's? That's speculation. I don't know if he would have spent a lot of money or not. I imagine he would have spent more money than the Fishers. The Fishers haven't changed their ways since they bought the team. They're billionaires and aren't spending as much as I did. I'm not picking on the Fishers, but they're going the other way and, I believe, spending less than we were, relative to the times. I don't know, they might be spending more, but don't forget that they were getting millions and millions in revenue sharing, and we didn't get any of that. We had the team before full revenue sharing kicked in. Some of it was trickling in, but we were making pennies on the dollar compared with what the Fishers made in revenue sharing.

Peter Guber, who became Lacob's partner with the Warriors, had made a couple of earlier inquiries about the A's, in both 1999 and 2001, with another partner, Paul Schaeffer, his filmmaker friend. Nothing came of their interest in 1999, but a couple of other groups pursued the team at that time, back when the Coliseum board had the authority to force a sale. We hadn't had a winning season yet and still were finding it tough to draw at the Coliseum but didn't want to sell. The Coliseum board was open to listening to groups making bids, and I was really upset about it. We had to fight like hell to make sure it didn't happen.

One group was led by Robert Piccinini of Modesto, who ran the Save Mart and Lucky supermarkets and later became a minority owner in the Warriors under Lacob and Guber. Piccinini was putting a full-court press on us to sell and was ready to pay $122 million. His group included Hall of Famer Joe Morgan, George Zimmer of Men's Wearhouse, and Andy Dolich, who was the front man and had headed the A's marketing department during the Haas ownership. Joe eventually backed out to focus on broadcasting, and Reggie Jackson came in. The other group was led by Michael Lazarus, an attorney and banker from San Mateo, and involved Arizona developer Lyle Campbell; Steve Stone, a broadcaster in Chicago and former Giants pitcher; and Bob Watson, the former first baseman/outfielder and Yankees GM.

Again, we didn't want to sell at that point, but these groups were being signed off on by the Coliseum board, which preferred the Piccinini group because it was more local. Both groups were shot down by Major League Baseball. Bud had launched a blue-ribbon task force to study the game's economic problems and said no team would be sold until the study was over. That pretty much ended that talk, which was fine with us. All our work was beginning to pay off. We had a winning season in 1999, the start of a prosperous stretch in A's history. We made the playoffs the next four years with one of the best teams in the game.

"We had the money. Bob Piccinini was well-heeled in supermarkets, and we had others who'd join the group. Bud and baseball had a plan for two teams to be contracted, and there was going to be a dispersal draft. The contraction plan, more than anything else, is what it came down to with our pursuit. That was their main focus. Steve and Ken kept the team. Through it all, Steve and those around him were straightforward and very professional."

—Andy Dolich

Guber's name surfaced again in 2001, but that was mostly just talk that he and Schaeffer, who founded Mandalay Sports Entertainment, were interested in buying for $150 million. It never amounted to anything. There were conversations—again, it's prudent to listen—but nothing was finalized. That was about the time I was trying to move the team down to Santa Clara and trying to deal with Bud on what he considered territorial rights for the Giants in the South Bay, which included both Santa Clara and San Jose. There was a lot of talk at one point that we were interested in moving the team to Las Vegas, but we never wanted to move out of the Bay Area. I was not interested in going to Las Vegas. That never got serious. Plus, Major League Baseball didn't think it was a big enough market and was not in favor of it anyway, because of the gambling. That was long before baseball brought in MGM and other betting companies as sponsors. Las Vegas now has a football team, hockey team, and soccer team and is confident it could land a baseball team and is wooing the Fishers.

Lew Wolff, who was Bud's friend, came into the picture late in our ownership as a stadium consultant and was the front man for the Fishers. Bud wanted Lew to help us with the ballpark pursuit and asked me to take him on and consider him in the acquisition. Lew wasn't going to buy it by himself. He wanted someone else to carry the big burden, and he ended up partnering with the Fishers. Lew later tried to get a ballpark in Fremont and San Jose, but it never materialized. You want a stadium closer to BART like it is right now.

Reggie Jackson had a group that he said wanted to buy the team, with Brian Shapiro and other investors, and said they were willing to pay $25 million more than what the Fishers were offering. But by the time Reggie contacted me, we had the deal in place. It would have been great and historic for Reggie to be part of the ownership group, as the first African American owner. I had a good relationship with Reggie, having retired his No. 9 a year earlier. But I had to commit to the deal with the Fishers and baseball and couldn't chase the last dollar.

As for Lacob and Guber, they later bought the Warriors for a bit more than they were considering buying the A's for: $450 million.

"I've had a standing offer to buy the A's from John Fisher for I don't even know how long. Over a decade. It's up to him; it's his business. It would have been smarter to sell to me a long time ago because we would have been partners, and he would have been able to own a part of the Warriors as well. I tried to tell him that. I would have done a ratio deal. You've seen the increase in value we've created by building a stadium and building the business. I do think it's sad that we didn't get the A's over any time in the last 17 years. I think we would've done a really good job with the A's. But look, obviously I'm biased."

—Joe Lacob

"There was a lot of drama around the Oakland franchise, but not because of Steve. I liked Steve. He was a good owner. He was cooperative and reasonable and great with me. He loved the game, loved the franchise. In a lot of ways, I didn't want to see him go. When he was selling, obviously, I knew Lew well and John Fisher well. At some point in life, you've got to decide and make a qualitative judgment in the best interest of the game. Nothing against Joe Lacob. I thought John Fisher and Lew Wolff would be a great combination."

—Bud Selig

Chapter 33

Why I Sold

IN THE DECADE THAT WE OWNED THE A's, we had our share of ups and downs. From losing 97 games in 1997 to reaching the playoffs four straight years to dropping the first-round series every year—each time pushing the series to the limit before falling in the fifth game—to building up fan interest, attendance, and the farm system.

It was an amazing emotional ride, and we did what we set out to do when buying the team. We were determined to keep the team in the Bay Area, and we did. We didn't get a stadium built, and that was frustrating because we tried different ways to find a home superior to the Coliseum. Even with the subpar stadium and the unfortunate Mount Davis situation that was dealt to us with the unexpected return of the Raiders, we made vast improvements with the help of so many people in and out of baseball.

Our first year, we drew 1.1 million fans, and that figure spiked to 2.2 million by the end. Without revenues that other teams generated from their newer baseball-only ballparks, we didn't have the payroll to justify re-signing Jason Giambi or Miguel Tejada and others—or match the bids they got elsewhere—though we tried on some fronts. We did sign Eric Chavez to a contract that's still the largest in franchise history, and we were able to replenish the minor league system and develop some top young talent, notably a rotation of aces: Tim Hudson, Mark Mulder, and Barry Zito, who made all those playoff runs possible.

As an owner of a baseball team, I looked at myself as a proud caretaker of a public trust. I knew it wasn't forever. A decade was a good length of time. With my business, I always had to keep a balance while either giving full attention to the A's or putting the right people in charge but always remaining available to work things out. The A's are more than a century old, founded in Philadelphia in 1901 as a charter member of the American League, and it was a privilege to be the franchise's fifth ownership group. That was enough for me to carry the torch. Eventually, it was time to pass it on.

"I wish Steve would've enjoyed it more when he was here, enjoyed some of the good times more. I think I said that to him once. The Haas family was a tough act to follow, but the game and the business were changing in the mid-'90s. I think he put a lot of pressure on himself being the owner of the team. I think he wanted to win every game.

"Steve always seemed a little bit uncomfortable in the public eye, but there were times he did enjoy it. I remember shortly after he bought the team, we took Ken's plane to the Dominican Republic—me, Sandy, Steve, Ken. We were there a few days to see our new complex. Sandy and Karl Kuehl were really proud of it. It was one of the first, behind the Dodgers and Toronto, and I remember Steve having a great time. He loosened up, was laughing, had a lot of fun. You saw that side of him. It was great to see. It was a blast. I hope he looks back and realizes he was an owner of a pretty good baseball team. From 2000 to 2003, we had the most wins of any four years in A's history, a pretty impressive run with great teams, back-to-back 100-win seasons, and it was tough to beat that 2001 team. Hopefully Steve looks

back and realizes he helped put it all together. He was at the top of the organization and deserves credit."

—Billy Beane

Ken Hofmann and I sold the A's in spring training of 2005 to the Fishers for $180 million. I don't think I would have ever sold if I didn't have a partner who a lot of times second-guessed me. That's just the way it was. We had to argue with him a lot to do this, do that. He was all over the map, and I got tired of that. I thought if there was an opportunity to get out, I better get out. He was getting older. I didn't know who I'd deal with if something happened to him. So we sold. Sometimes how you plan things on paper isn't how they work out in real life. He was very much the opposite of me. He didn't like to make decisions and have to stick with them. He might make a decision one day but want to change it the next day. He was unpredictable. That was hard to deal with because if I made a decision, that was that—I stuck with it. He was pecking away as a Monday morning quarterback, yet I was doing the work as the managing partner while half of everything was going to go to him. He wasn't happy with what I did or didn't do.

There was a lot of stress, and I was also running my company, so I thought it was time to sell. I wasn't going to be able to find another partner because Hofmann was going to sell only if I sold. That was the sort of thing we were up against.

It was hard to part with the team because we were improving our reputation as an organization; we were far more successful than in the first years we took over. I was glad we gave a lot of young players a chance that they might not have received elsewhere. The team we inherited had a lot of older players, and we changed that. Early on, I told Sandy Alderson, "We need to bring in more good, young pitchers."

Our actions weren't always appreciated by fans or the press. Some in the press didn't do us many favors and thought we were cheapskates and weren't trying to promote the team. It was a tough deal. Especially those early years. We got beaten up pretty good. But we had a plan, which was to rebuild the franchise through the farm system, turn it into an annual contender with young players leading the way, and make it entertaining for fans to rally around. In a lot of ways, we did that.

> *"Steve showed a lot of patience with the team. He realized it would take a while to get where we got. He enjoyed coming to games and talking baseball. The fact he did play some ball when he was younger probably allowed him to understand the game more than a lot of owners who are very wealthy and can afford to buy a team."*
>
> —Art Howe

Now, I must say, if I had known franchise values would have soared the way they did, I might not have sold. Hindsight is 20/20, of course, but Major League Baseball did well for itself with MLB Advanced Media, which oversees baseball's online presence, along with MLB Network, MLB.com, and all the other resources that generate millions and millions of dollars of revenue. After we sold, those numbers were beginning to jump. When we owned the team, it wasn't easy with our budget, revenues, and rising salaries. There wasn't much profit, and the profit we made would stay in the operation.

Revenue sharing was in the embryonic stage and turned out to be a bonanza for the Fishers, but I didn't cry over it. I wanted out. It was time. We sometimes had a tough road during the ownership, but the experience was an honor and thrill, and I was proud of what we accomplished and delivered to the fans and community.

Long Schott

"The A's have had six ownership groups since they were founded in 1901, and the highest winning percentage was during the Schott-Hofmann years at .540. The franchise's time in Oakland has been very successful, but much like in Philadelphia, the teams were either very bad or very good. Likewise, the A's were bad the first three years under Schott and Hofmann, but the next six years, '99 through '04, were terrific."

—David Feldman, A's historian

Chapter 34

A Future Stadium

I ALWAYS THOUGHT IF THE A's were going to stay in the East Bay, the perfect place to build a ballpark and prosper for the long term in Oakland was the Coliseum parking lot. Right at the site the A's have played since moving to the Bay Area in 1968.

The Fishers are trying to build a stadium at Howard Terminal on the waterfront near Jack London Square, but to go over there and disturb the environment where the port is, where the steel plant is, where all those workers are—I think it's absolutely crazy. There's too much opposition over there. You've got the shipyard against you. You've got the unions against you. I wouldn't be fooling around with that.

Major League Baseball is siding with A's ownership, which also is being romanced in Las Vegas. The Fishers are considering relocation and leaving the area, something I wouldn't have wanted to do. I don't know why they don't just build where they are now. Tear down the Coliseum and put up their 35,000-seat ballpark and ballpark village right there. It'll eventually come down anyway. You've got the freeways that pass right by. You've got Bay Area Rapid Transit that runs right by. It has a lot of potential. Everything is right there. It's central. All you've got to do is solve the traffic issues with new infrastructure. You shouldn't have contamination cleanup like you'd have at the terminal. Concerns seem endless at Howard Terminal, especially if you exclude yourself from BART.

"Robert Bobb was the city manager and wanted to build a stadium for the A's downtown, and Jerry Brown was the mayor and didn't care about the A's. A study was commissioned for almost half a million dollars for seven different sites. The most difficult, most expensive, and most troublesome was Howard Terminal. So years later, when the A's picked the Howard Terminal site, they knew it was going to fail. Then Major League Baseball announced the A's could explore other markets. To me, it was a setup from the get-go. It's a very sad scenario for this mayor and city council, which could lose three teams within a few years. I blame them. Oakland had three sports franchises and thousands of jobs. Everybody knows the best site is right there at the Coliseum, which seems irrelevant at this point."
—Ignacio De La Fuente, former Oakland city council president

We didn't have the option of rebuilding at the Coliseum because the Raiders and Warriors were still on the property. There was no room for a baseball stadium in the parking lot. We couldn't have had three buildings in that space. We thought about it, but it was never an option with the other tenants present. Now the other teams are gone, the Raiders to Las Vegas and the Warriors to San Francisco, and the A's have the land to themselves. You don't have to deal with two franchises that were competition for you. You could build your privately financed park on the premises. In this world today, I don't see how you get a park built without using your own money, at least in California. No one's getting a free stadium.

They could have their ballpark village on the site and do wonders to help revive that part of town. Bars, restaurants, housing—with a 35,000-seat ballpark as the crown jewel. That's what has hurt the Coliseum, all that extra seating. You can't sell season tickets when you know there always will be available seating.

You can't always fill 50,000 or 60,000 seats, so putting together a more intimate park would make more sense. That's what we wanted to build in Santa Clara, where the 49ers play now, but there was that roadblock called territorial rights. At the time, because of the Raiders and Warriors, we couldn't build at the Coliseum site, but they can do it now. I would do it now.

While most teams built nice ballparks in the 1990s and early 2000s, all with their own traits and character, the A's remain at their original facility and have the fifth-oldest stadium in the majors. Fenway Park and Wrigley Field are shrines that were built in the early 1900s, and Dodger Stadium opened in 1962. Then there is Anaheim Stadium, which has benefited from all its upgrades. Then the Coliseum, where you haven't seen those upgrades. The only significant change in 50-some years, and it wasn't for the better, was the construction of Mount Davis, an eyesore that destroyed the baseball atmosphere and character. It's no secret the A's need a new home to compete against the bigger teams and secure their best players. The Bay Area would be supporting two thriving franchises. The Giants wouldn't own the market on nice facilities.

The A's could keep playing at their building during construction of a new one next door. Plenty of new ballparks were built alongside existing facilities that were being replaced. It happened in Chicago at the site of Comiskey Park. It happened in New York at both Yankee Stadium and Shea Stadium. It happened in Arlington, St. Louis, Cincinnati, Atlanta, and Philadelphia. It's a long list, and they all worked. Shoot, we know what it's like to play with ongoing construction. It happened right in front of us during our games when they were putting the finishing touches on Mount Davis. It wouldn't be as bad playing while a new stadium is under construction next door in the parking lot. The property is plenty big to make it work.

> "Since the Warriors moved out and the Raiders left, maybe there's some practicality to building it on the current site. I still believe baseball stadiums do better in downtown locations. You're competing, remember, with the Giants, who have a jewel of a ballpark on the waterfront. But having said all that, if you couldn't do Howard Terminal for some reason, I do believe for the first time in many years maybe it could be done at the Coliseum site because you're the only sports team in town. Like Steve's view. And build a ballpark village all around the site and create a destination.
>
> "I really like John. I hope he's successful. It's very difficult to get anything done in the Bay Area. They wanted infrastructure funding. Even that, I would've had this thing done a long time ago. I'd just pay for it all privately like I did with the Warriors. And you know what? You get to say at the end of the day, 'I didn't take any money from you.' You didn't get the $300 million or $400 million in infrastructure money, whatever, but it's easier for me to be able to take that tack. I think it's the right thing in this world, in this place. I would've just gone and done it. Think of all the revenue you would've gotten if you had done it 10 years ago. Sometimes people want to strike the best deal, but this isn't a business like any other. They know the numbers better than I do for their situation, but sometimes you've just got to get it done."
>
> —Joe Lacob

The A's have discussed building a village on the Coliseum site to help fund the project at Howard Terminal, but building the park at the Coliseum would fund itself, and the village would accompany the park, not be separate from it. It makes obvious sense. It's a logical space.

Part Six

SUCCEEDING IN BUSINESS

Chapter 35

The Lesson of Sticking with It

LIKE IN BASEBALL, IF YOU GET KNOCKED DOWN in business, you've got to pick yourself up, dust yourself off, and take another shot. And keep doing it until you hit the ball out of the park again and again.

When I was young, I got terminated from two homebuilding companies but didn't let it get to me. I knew what I was doing. I liked what I was doing. If you feel passionate about a certain line of work, don't give up if someone puts up a roadblock. In my case, it happened twice.

Coming out of the military, my first job was as a cost accountant at Ford Motor Company. I spent a year with Ford and couldn't stand it. I mastered the job in three months and was looking for more work and was told just to look busy and not to worry about it. But I'm not the kind of guy who could do that. I concluded I didn't want to work at a big corporation. It wasn't that I was working the assembly line that never stops, and when it does, you're yelled at. "Why did it stop? We're losing money." I worked as an assistant to the superintendent and sat in an office and did clerical work. A secretary, for lack of a better word. It turned me off. Anyone who wanted to take a big leap in the company had to move to Dearborn, Michigan. A kid like me living in California knew nothing about Dearborn, Michigan. I never asked. Thank God. I might have been talked into moving.

I was very enthusiastic. I wanted to conquer the world, be successful and, of course, make big money. In high school and college, I had worked summers on survey crews that did the topographic work for housing developments, including boundaries and future lot lines. I was a rear chainman and worked for a couple of civil engineering firms, MacKay & Somps, which was founded back in 1953, and the Nolte Company, a competitor. I was getting union pay because of a special union code that allowed for students in school who got summer jobs to get union pay at a somewhat reduced scale. I worked every summer except the summer I played ball in Canada. So when I was at Ford and wanted to get out, I spoke with my brother, Larry, and told him, "I've got to find something else." He's the one who directed me into the building and land-developing business.

I always told Larry, "If not for you, I wouldn't be where I am today." He was so influential in my career, always helped me, always looked out for me. He did a lot of design work for builders and had been a civil engineer at MacKay & Somps and eventually became its first partner. When I told him I would leave Ford, he helped me get an interview at the American Housing Guild. I got the job, a beginner's position. They were a small start-up from Southern California that didn't last very long, and they had opened an operation in the Bay Area, but they decided to go in a different direction and laid off a bunch of people. I was one of them. After a year, I was terminated but not about to give up.

A couple of weeks later, I got my next job at Duc & Elliot Builders, which was challenging and rewarding, and I was learning the business and getting to know people. I gained valuable experience in all aspects of land acquisitions, land planning, and homebuilding. When people at the company were out or sick, I became an agent able to meet with contractors to get bids for underground work such as storm drains, sanitation, water, grading, paving, and gas and electric. I did everything from A to Z. They didn't have financial capital and had to borrow through the nose all the time. They did business on a shoestring, and I didn't like that. Elliot was the builder, and Duc was the promoter, the dealmaker, and also a playboy who conducted much of his business in a bar.

I was learning a lot doing everything from serving as a runner and purchase agent to working with banks and lining up subcontractors. The job was slow and boring, but the downtime gave me an opportunity to earn my real estate license so I could sell houses. I worked on the side to build two spec houses, which are houses based on market value but without a buyer and built on speculation that people will buy once they're completed. I needed money because Duc & Elliot paid diddly. I started at $600 a month and then got up to $950 a month. The most I made was $1,000, and I was there five years. So I went to a bank manager who gave me a construction loan—the lots were $5,000—and built a spec house and then another one in Los Gatos that we moved into because we had a growing family.

Someone I met while at Duc & Elliot was a fellow named Ellery Williams, who sold me windows. He was a very good football player at Santa Clara, an end, and played briefly for the New York Giants. Ellery was the nicest, friendliest guy you'd ever want to meet. I didn't know this at first, but he began talking about his brother, who was Dick Williams, the Hall of Fame manager. I always found it interesting that

Ellery was so cordial and laid-back while Dick was a quick-tempered guy who never was afraid to chew someone out. But Dick was successful managing and won back-to-back World Series championships for the A's long before I was involved with the team.

In the early 1970s, I was offered a job at William Lyon Homes, a public company that was a lot larger, with more capital. William Lyon was a major general and chief of the Air Force Reserve who became an extremely successful homebuilder. I spent five years at William Lyon, a good job, and got promoted to general manager of the San Ramon operation but told them I couldn't make that long drive for the same wage. I wound up making $1,500 a month or $18,000 a year, plus mileage. I was actually making more than my boss, Dick Randall, who resented the fact that I got a raise. I guess I was a threat, so he ended up terminating me.

The day I got dismissed from the American Housing Guild, I came home early and my wife asked why. I said I got fired. Same thing happened years later at William Lyon. I came home early and explained I got let go. It got to the point where whenever I came home early from work, she'd say, "Oh, my God, what happened?" The firings had nothing to do with my ability. They were for unjust reasons. Naturally, I wanted to prove everybody wrong. Later, at a homebuilders conference in San Francisco, I had a meeting with General Bill Lyon. We met at the Fairmont. He said he had been sorry to see me go, and he and I left on the best of terms.

"I got to know Steve well when we lived near each other while he was working at Ford Motor Company. Everything he did, he did on his own, which was impressive. He didn't have a lot of money. No silver spoon. He got what he worked for. Nobody handed him much. He made it on his own and has been very

generous donating to Bellarmine, St. Francis, Santa Clara, and various charities."

—Ron Calcagno, former Santa Clara quarterback and catcher, football coach at St. Francis High School in the Bay Area, and employee in the A's community relations department

As it turned out, Dick Randall did me a favor because leaving William Lyon allowed me to take one of the biggest steps of my career: I began working for Singer Housing Company, which was merging with the development company Besco around that time. Besco was one of California's top homebuilders in the 1950s and 1960s, owned by Wayne Valley and Jack Brooks, who became managers of Singer Housing. Jack knew me from the industry. He was a major Democratic supporter and ally of Jerry Brown, and heavy into East Bay politics, and I had gone to quite a few political functions to know what was going on for my own job. I guess I made an impression on Jack because he liked me and thought I was pretty sharp. He's the one who introduced me and recommended me to Wayne.

I remember my interview like it was yesterday. Wayne said, "Well, Schott, we want tigers around here, no pussycats. We want people who can get it done now." I said, "Don't worry about it. I won't be a pussycat. I'll get it done the right way and promptly."

Chapter 36

Moving up the Ladder

EVERYTHING CHANGED FOR ME when I began working at Singer Housing Company for Wayne Valley and Jack Brooks, the biggest builders in Northern California by far. Singer Housing was a subsidiary of the corporation that made Singer sewing machines and thought it could get into the homebuilding business and make a lot of money and shore up its sewing machine business, which was heading downward. It wasn't that easy.

When I was starting at Singer, I discovered something they were doing that wasn't smart. Jack asked me to start taking over more duties for him, and one was to start doing cost analysis and house appraisals. Surprisingly, here's how they figured how to price a house: combine all costs to build and add 10 percent. They weren't pricing their homes to the market, which is what they should have been doing. You want to be competitive, but you don't want to give it away either. You need to understand what the market is. It was an exercise in futility. I told them it had to be changed. We should be doing it another way for better profit. It just made sense. Everybody does it that way today. But at the time, the Bay Area housing market was changing rapidly, and people were trying to figure it out.

My parents, Edgar and Mary, on their wedding day. They grew up in Petaluma and settled in Santa Clara, where my father was its first city engineer.

Before I wanted to be a Major League Baseball player, my childhood dream was to be a farmer. We lived on a prune orchard, and my grandparents ran a chicken ranch. I loved the outdoors, the open land.

I played high school ball at Bellarmine College Prep in San Jose and was fortunate to be named Player of the Year and All-City by the *San Jose Mercury*.

At Santa Clara University, we advanced to the NCAA tournament my junior year. Here I'm sitting with (left to right) Bill Renna, an All-American at Santa Clara who played six seasons in the majors, including with the 1953 World Series–champion Yankees; Len Scarpelli, who played before me at Santa Clara; Henry Schmidt, the longtime Santa Clara trainer; and Bob Fatjo, my high school coach.

The Lethbridge White Sox, my summer college team in Canada. I'm standing second from left, next to Gary Kirk, who ran the team. Ray Washburn, who pitched for the Cardinals and no-hit the Giants at Candlestick Park a day after Gaylord Perry no-hit the Cardinals, is in the back row fourth from left. My buddy Dick Creighton is in the back row third from right.

I served in the Army Reserve for six years, starting with basic training at Fort Ord and active duty at Fort Gordon, where I graduated as a military policeman.

My brother, Larry, was 7½ years older than I, and my sister, Dianne, was 18 months older than him. Despite the age difference, they were always there for me.

Pat and I were married in 1962. Our three children, left to right, are Lisa, Steve, and Kristen.

Our grandkids were huge A's fans and loved going to games. Matt, Michael, and Robert are in the front row and Trever, Nick, Ryan, and Kenny are in the back row.

Over the years, we've built and sold more than 40,000 homes, specializing in starter homes. That's a thrilling part, helping to make dreams come true for first-time homebuyers.

Wayne Valley, an extremely successful homebuilder, was my mentor and eventually my partner. He's also the man who brought Al Davis to the Raiders.

I'll always cherish my friendship with Yogi Berra and the times we and our wives had together.

Pat and I attended the Kentucky Derby a couple of times. They were unforgettable visits—including our time with Jimmy the Greek, the legendary bookmaker.

After I was recruited to buy the A's, I served as owner and managing general partner from 1995 to 2005. We reached the postseason in four straight years.

My partner with the A's, Ken Hofmann, with our wives, Pat and Jean, along with the team mascot, Stomper.

Mark McGwire was our biggest draw in our first season with the A's. He hit 52 home runs and two years later set the single-season record in St. Louis. Sandy Alderson was our general manager.

My mother's favorite player was Miguel Tejada, who's looking over his daughter Alexa and my granddaughter Brinley on the Oakland Coliseum grass.

Broadcaster Bill King was a hero to me. I got hooked at a young age with his Raiders calls, but he was excellent calling the A's and Warriors too. The revered voice of Oakland.

I didn't often visit the clubhouse; that was the players' turf. But as an old pitcher, I enjoyed hearing from the guys who made their living on the mound.

One of my proudest moments as A's owner was getting Reggie Jackson's No. 9 retired. His only wish was to donate money to Oakland schools, and we gladly got it done.

I have much respect for Tony La Russa—not just for his Hall of Fame career in baseball but for his work at his Animal Rescue Foundation, which I've happily supported since day one.

One of my very special friends, Gary Kirk (center), ran my summer baseball team in Canada and years later introduced me to his best friend, Wayne Newton. Gary, Wayne, and I enjoyed good times together, including aboard my plane.

I've had a number of planes and helicopters over the years, which turned out to be a great benefit to my business and also a valuable resource to help people and share with others.

I was invited to throw the ceremonial first pitch before the initial game at Santa Clara University's baseball stadium, one of the country's top college baseball complexes. I was privileged to fund the facility and have the school name it after me.

With some of my many friends from the Santa Clara class of 1960 (left to right): John Sobrato, who was instrumental in the development of Silicon Valley and appears on the Forbes 400 list; Leon Panetta, former White House chief of staff, secretary of defense, and CIA director; and Everett Alvarez Jr., an American hero who was the first U.S. fighter pilot shot down over Vietnam and a prisoner of war for more than eight years.

Pat and I visited the Vatican and had an unforgettable moment with Pope John Paul II, who gave us his special blessing.

I was fortunate to play golf with President Gerald Ford, who I must say is a hacker like the rest of us. That evening, we dined with our wives, Pat and Betty.

It was an honor to be acknowledged by President George W. Bush after receiving the prestigious Horatio Alger Award. In a speech, he singled me out as a suffering baseball owner, which got laughs because everyone knew he had owned the Rangers before I bought the A's.

As a Horatio Alger Award recipient, I was given a beautiful medallion. But more than that, it's about further committing to helping young people get educations through need-based college scholarship programs.

Among the Horatio Alger Santa Clara University Schott Family Scholarship recipients: Jennifer Cuevas (far left), Morgan Fleshren (second from left), Martimeano Villa (second from right), and George Shappell (far right). I'm alongside Pat and former university president Father Michael Engh.

Sitting peacefully with Pat and our beloved nine-pound Norwich Terrier, Sadie.

Say the total cost of building a house was $60,000. It sounds silly now, but that was the price range of homes back then. Add 10 percent, and the sale price was just $66,000. It was a fixed formula and had nothing to do with the market. Small house or big house, it didn't matter. They weren't taking the time to check the market. They were selling houses so quickly that they weren't making the profits they should have been making. After I spoke up, we put an end to that thinking and started making a lot more money from home sales. Not that I came up with anything magical, just a better formula for doing something to generate more profit. It was about considering the market, the geography, the square footage and pricing the home accordingly. At the same time, we always tried to sell a bit below market so we could have an edge over the competition.

Another thing I tried to improve was our marketing. We weren't very good at it. In fact, we were pretty bad. The model homes weren't kept up. The floor plans were good, but we didn't show them well or market them well. At the time, we were building houses like crazy. The first year at Singer, my geographic area was Santa Clara County, the Peninsula, and Alameda County, and another partner was in Contra Costa County. Jack told Wayne that I was capable of doing more than I was doing, and I started moving up the ladder and buying land in San Jose for the company because they thought I was pretty good at it, and I liked it.

After a year and a half, I got promoted. Jack and Wayne didn't freely throw around titles. I was vice president at previous companies, but the jobs paid peanuts. That was the consolation the company gave you: better titles. At Singer, I was paid far more without the title, so I didn't care about titles.

As it turned out, Singer didn't last long in the homebuilding business. It concluded it required too much capital to survive and didn't believe it could afford to stay in the industry. Indeed, you've got to buy the land, you've got to do the prep work, you've got to build the homes. It takes time. You want your company to build up assets. That wasn't Singer's strength. In 1977, with Jack retired, Wayne had a chance to gain full control of the company. Big corporations like that don't like cash tied up in land, and Singer decided to get out. The stock wasn't doing well, and Wayne said, "Shucks, if I can buy it at the right price, I'll try to buy it back." So he purchased Singer Housing, and I bought a small interest. It was renamed Citation Homes and initially divided into three geographic areas among Dennis Cheney, Tony Allen, and me. We were minority partners.

That was a pretty big year for me. I used to say to myself, "Wouldn't it be cool to make a million dollars?" It's not an uncommon dream, right? That year, it came true. It was something I thought about but didn't know would happen. When it did, I couldn't believe it. Not like I had a million dollars in my hand. It was tied up in the company. It was a piece of paper showing the amount. Still, it was so exciting considering my wife and I had just $500 between us when we got married.

It eventually became Wayne and me, and while Wayne received 74 percent of the corporation's earnings, I got 18 percent, plus 8 percent that Wayne was holding back so I wouldn't jump ship. There was an agreement with Wayne that as soon as I built 7,600 homes myself, it would be an equal partnership, and we'd share the profits 50-50. Not the equity but the profits. It took a lot of hard work to reach that goal. He wanted to structure the deal so we'd stick around a while. He had gotten burned previously by other guys, such as Al Davis, and wanted to make sure he didn't get burned again. He had a lot of stake in us. He didn't want to give us equal partnership until we proved we were able.

I say "we" because I always needed people to get to where I got; it wasn't about "I, I, I." Anyone who tells you he does it all by himself is full of BS. I wasn't the one building those homes. We had crews doing everything. We became the biggest builder in California and stayed No. 1 for a long time, one year building more than 3,000 homes. We were in the top 10 in the U.S. for several years, and thanks to all the people who contributed to what we accomplished and the strong foundation we set, I was inducted into the Homebuilders Hall of Fame by the California Homebuilding Foundation at a 2004 ceremony in San Francisco. The CHF is a nonprofit laying the ground for scholastic success for future builders in the state, and I donated to their scholarships. I'm quoted on the website as saying, "Only with a strong foundation will you have success," and that applies in both homebuilding and life.

"Steve definitely has a sixth sense. He sees things other people don't and has that innate ability to determine these things and stay on top of these things. Plus he's very disciplined and thorough, probably the most disciplined man I ever met. He remained disciplined when spending attention to detail. He'll call me on things that might appear to be minutiae, but being on top of things is one of Steve's strengths."

—Dan Ikeda, chief financial officer,
SCS Development Company

For me, Wayne figured it would take 10 years to build the 7,600 homes, so he projected the term to be 10 years, but it took seven and a half. That made it 50-50—a huge difference, of course, going from 18 percent of every dollar to 50 percent. I was able to make more money. It was accruing, and it was there when he died in 1986. Eventually I bought out Wayne's interest. I had a good amount of capital from the corporation, so I could use the liquidity to borrow from banks and pay off his estate. At the time he died, he had two-thirds ownership and I had one-third. It was a five-year payoff. It was quite a bit different for me compared with early in my career when I was building houses for my family and had no equity or financial standing that a bank would consider.

Over the years, I had my share of runs-ins with Wayne. He was a tough son of a gun. I don't mean that disrespectfully, but sometimes I'd tell him, "Damn it, you always want more and are never happy with what I do." I wasn't scared of him. I was reporting to Wayne until he changed it up and told me I had to report to a new marketing guy he had hired. The guy didn't know more than I did, and probably knew less. I was pissed off, but I had been in the Army and understood chain of command.

Anyway, one time Wayne came down to my office and started asking questions about a project. I stopped him and told him I couldn't talk to him anymore. Chain of command, right? Wayne called me a wiseass, took a lit cigar from his mouth, and threw the friggin' thing at me. It was going to hit me in the face. Well, I guess my baseball instincts kicked in. I caught it in my palm, and it burned my hand. I threw it back and hit him right on his forehead, and it bounced onto the floor. My office had a big glass window that all the workers could see through. They were saying, "Oh, Schott's gone by the end of the week." They were taking bets. But I didn't fear for my job. Being let go from two previous jobs didn't change my opinion. I was confident in my abilities. I wasn't that high in the pecking order then, but Wayne thought I had some talent. After I threw the cigar at him, all I heard back was, "You've got quick hands." He laughed it off. I said, "I was a pitcher. If I didn't have quick hands, I'd have a lot of bruises and broken bones with all the line drives hit back at me."

We kept the name Citation Homes, which was recognized as a top-notch builder. Citation no longer exists. We dissolved it years ago, and we're SCS Development Company—my initials: Steve Charles Schott.

These days, we're largely working on developing apartments and have a subsidiary company, Award Homes.

I really enjoyed what I was doing with Wayne and had to jump around to different jobs, but that's OK. The engineers, real estate brokers, landowners, architects, subcontractors, attorneys, people I dealt with at different levels, including the title companies—I enjoyed every aspect of it. I met a lot of fine people. Some not so fine. The more I did, the more I liked it. I got into both land development and homebuilding because that's how you make your largest profits. I would have limited myself if I had done one or the other. I wanted the upside of buying the land and building on it. Did I have visions of becoming a major builder and building more than 40,000 homes? No. I had no clue. I just figured if I did things the right way, had some luck, wasn't reckless, didn't act like a big shot, and just focused on my game plan, it would work out in the long run, and it did.

Chapter 37

Wayne Valley, My Mentor and the Man Who Hired Al Davis...Twice

LOOKING BACK, WITH WAYNE VALLEY wildly successful in the homebuilding industry, I was fortunate to work for him and later partner with him. Wayne was an influential factor in my life and career and the man who hired Al Davis to coach the Oakland Raiders.

Wayne was one of eight original owners of the Raiders when they debuted in the old American Football League in 1960, and a big part of the AFL's early growth. Wayne and Ed McGah became the primary owners of the Raiders, and Wayne, a big, strong guy who was a star football player at Oregon State, served as the managing general partner. Al Davis was an assistant coach with the Chargers when Wayne hired him to coach the Raiders in 1963, and after Al left to become AFL commissioner for a short spell in 1966, Wayne brought him back as a partner with a 10 percent stake in the team and title as head of football operations.

Wayne and Al might have gotten along at the beginning but not for long. Al went around him and got McGah to go along with him. Two years after the 1970 NFL-AFL merger, Davis took control of the Raiders' operations and pushed Wayne aside. By California law, if two of the three partners had agreed on the change, it was ratified, and Davis and McGah voted in favor of Davis. So Wayne was left out. He tried to overturn the ruling in court but got rejected and sold his stake in the team in 1976. Interestingly, Wayne tried to buy the 49ers right around that time, but Davis found a way to put up a roadblock, thanks to his association with Warriors owner Franklin Mieuli, who owned a small piece of the 49ers. Davis got Mieuli to exercise his first refusal right of any 49ers sale, which blocked the purchase to Valley even though Mieuli never was going to buy the team. Nevertheless, it ended Valley's bid to buy the 49ers and led to Eddie DeBartolo acquiring the team.

I became a Raiders fan, not necessarily more than a 49ers fan— the Raiders were so fun to watch in the 1970s—and went to a lot of games because of my connection with Wayne and Jack Brooks, another cofounder of the Raiders, though he held on to his shares much longer. Brooks often offered me tickets, and I attended the Sea of Hands game in which Ken Stabler led the Raiders to a playoff win in December 1974 with a last-minute pass in the end zone to Clarence Davis, who fought off several defenders. I was with my son, who was 12 at the time, and we saw it so vividly from our view at the corner sideline, Stabler getting tackled as he desperately lofted the ball to Davis. One of the greatest games I ever saw.

I saw some wild games from the stands. My friends and business associates would go. Jack had a box at the Coliseum as one of the shareholders, and that was a lot of fun. People from Hollywood would come in the box and visit. I remember Jane Fonda, for one. She was very friendly and married at the time to the assemblyman Tom Hayden.

Wayne wouldn't sit in Jack's box. He preferred to sit outside with all the fans. Interestingly enough when Jack went to sell his shares, the only guy who could buy them was Al Davis, who didn't pay what they were worth even though the two were very close, so Jack didn't make as much money as he should have off that acquisition. Al was a conniver. A smart guy but ruthless. Wayne twice brought him to the Raiders, and Al didn't exactly repay the favor to Wayne.

I could see why Al and Wayne didn't always get along. Wayne was a taskmaster. But if I wouldn't have been able to connect with Wayne, I wouldn't be where I am today. He liked me a lot, but we had our disagreements. He and I thought a lot alike, at least in homebuilding. I think he thought of me like a son. But he was a tough guy and very difficult to work for. Sometimes he made it so miserable that I was ready to quit. Even when I was a partner, I wanted to quit. Pat told me not to because I'd give up too much. She encouraged me to hang in there and not give up. I respected my wife's opinions and didn't quit. It was nice to have her encouragement.

I didn't know I'd become a partner with Wayne, but it was a goal and dream come true. If I wanted to be my own operator, I had to be able to get involved with somebody who had money and could go to the bank for unlimited funds and pursue any project. When I was young, I thought the way to make what I called real money was to be part of an organization that made acquisitions like we did. To do it yourself and finance with the bank, you're taking all the risks. So many guys I knew went under because they couldn't get the financing. One little hiccup, and you could lose it all because of the up-and-down market, and people tend to buy houses when the interest rates are low. Wayne was the key guy for me. He opened the doors to my future.

Chapter 38

First-Time Homebuyers

I REMEMBER MY FIRST HOME PURCHASE like it was yesterday, even though it was in 1963, a couple of years after I graduated from college. Now, I didn't do much due diligence, which wasn't wise, but I was just happy at the time to have the opportunity to move my wife and our first two kids into a three-bedroom, two-bath, 1,300-square-foot house in an older area of San Jose.

The cost was $20,750, which doesn't sound like a lot now, but it was significant then. I had to qualify for an FHA loan. I finally did, though I had lost my job at the American Housing Guild while the loan was being processed. The FHA never found out. Fortunately, your employment isn't checked every day.

I didn't realize it when I bought the house, but our street backed up against a freeway—Highway 17, which runs south to Santa Cruz. Brokers never had to tell you anything like that back then. There weren't disclosures. When I moved in, I wondered where the noise came from. It wasn't that noisy during the day, but during the quiet of night, you could hear the cars as they passed by.

No matter. It was a thrill to be a first-time homeowner, to have a house under our feet and over our heads. In turn, when I got in a position to sell homes for a living, it was a great experience for me to be able to help make dreams come true for first-time homebuyers. I saw countless smiles on faces, people who were ecstatic to move into homes they could call their own. They were very satisfied, and in many cases, they sold their homes and made a lot of money because we had a good brand name.

Early on, I wanted to find out what it was like to sell houses, so I earned my real estate license and spent weekends showing houses. That was the first time I got a glimpse of people buying their first homes. These people earned the right. They built up good credit. They qualified for a loan. They came up with a down payment. Certain things had to come together for them, and to be able to buy their first home was a matter of pride, a big accomplishment in life, and I was delighted to help make it happen.

Over the years, we've built and sold more than 40,000 homes and specialized in first-time homes. Detached homes could be about 1,200 square feet, though as we grew, we started developing bigger homes, some as large as 3,000 square feet. For the most part, we wanted to make them inexpensive for first-time homebuyers. That was the game plan. We did just a small percentage of luxury homes.

Business wasn't always good, and we transitioned based on the times. In the late 1990s and early 2000s, when the market went soft and interest rates were high, we hit a brick wall. We considered all options and began focusing first on Salinas and then Soledad, towns in Monterey County where people might have commuted to San Jose. We wanted to remain on the low end of the market by making the houses as inexpensive as possible, starting in the low $200,000s. If the high-end market reached $400,000, we tried to be in the low $300,000s or high $200,000s.

One thing to note about Salinas and Soledad: We usually employed union subcontractors, but we had a difficult time finding them in Salinas and Soledad, so we received an exception to create our new company, Award Homes. That allowed us to employ nonunion contractors and build the homes so long as we never utilized that company in the Bay Area, where we hired union workers under SCS Development. It worked out well in Salinas and Soledad. A lot of people got quality lower-priced homes. Some investors might warn you not to buy houses when the market is bad, but there are reasons it works for the buyer. In Salinas and Soledad, we priced houses so reasonably that they were affordable in a down economy. We didn't know they'd sell, but they sold like hotcakes.

Creativity is essential to be successful in the industry. I remember a time back in the 1980s when rates were higher than 20 percent, making it difficult for buyers to qualify for loans, which made selling homes tough. We tried something different, a huge financial risk. I was working at Singer Housing with Wayne Valley, who came up with the idea of enabling homebuyers to obtain loans with an interest rate closer to 12 percent. We did this by acting as the lender for the buyers. Most loans generally were Federal Housing Administration or Veterans Affairs loans, meaning they were insured by the government. We partnered with Lindsey Mortgage, which collected payments as our loan servicer. In retrospect, it was risky because rates could have stayed high or increased, and we were selling loans far below market rate. We needed Singer's approval because it was so unusual. But the strategy allowed us to continue selling houses and make a profit. Eventually, rates came down and we were able to sell the loans at full value. So the gamble paid off. Not only did it allow us to continue selling homes through the adverse environment, but it allowed buyers who might not qualify for loans to qualify at lower rates.

Some projects are much tougher than others. Two immediately come to mind, from many years ago. In San Jose, we were trenching for PG&E lines, one of the final jobs before street paving, and uncovered Native American bones. Nobody had known it was a burial ground. There weren't laws covering such things at that point. But we contacted the authorities, who came in and said, "Wow, this is a big deal." They couldn't decide what to do with the bones. Our work was held up for almost a year, and the real estate market went in the tank. A lot of money was lost on the project. Eventually we got a judge's ruling, and the bones were able to be buried with a ceremony at an open-space area. Ours was the first such case. From that experience, a state law was passed to protect any Native American remains that are discovered at a construction site.

Another example came at Roberts Landing in San Leandro, the site of an old explosives manufacturing plant called the Trojan Powder Company, which closed in 1964. It's nearly 500 acres and sits along the shoreline of the bay. When I was with Wayne Valley, we purchased part of the property and were going to build a housing project, but then came the case of the salt marsh harvest mouse, an endangered species. We had to find a way to keep acreage available to preserve the mice. It was held up a long time, overlapping three mayors. With all the wetlands issues we had to resolve, it took us 20 years to get approval, and we could build on only 75 acres while more than 400 acres went to the city for open space. Normally on 500 acres, you can develop 2,500 to 3,000 houses, and we ended up with 700 lots. If we didn't agree on that, we'd still be out there trying for approval. Looking back, I'd say I was lucky to get that many units but disappointed because I thought it would be a lot more. This was at a time when homebuilding was a far simpler process. Today, I don't know if you could get anything approved at such a site.

"Invariably, especially these days, in the last 10 years, few projects are slam dunks, whether you're dealing in toxins or wetlands or endangered species. It's hard to find an easy piece of land to develop. It's always a challenge. That's part of Steve's strengths. He anticipates these challenges and pushes to get things done. He realizes, until you get permits, it's not a done deal, and he stresses to everyone in here to be diligent, alert, and thorough."

—Dan Ikeda

I mentioned that I lost my job at the American Housing Guild during the loan process for my first home, and I didn't even have a job when the loan was approved. But I was back working in two weeks with better pay at Duc & Elliot Builders. We lived at that San Jose house for five years and had our third child just before we sold it in 1967. It sold for around $24,000, a profit of a few thousand dollars. Appreciation was very low back then. You took what you got. I took it, bought a lot in Los Gatos for about $5,000, and took out another loan to build a house we lived in for 10 years. But you always remember your first house. It was a thrill for me, and it was a thrill to help make it possible for so many others.

Chapter 39

Air Travel

SPENDING MONEY CRAZILY IS SOMETHING I try not to do. I still drive a 1999 Mercedes because it's easy to drive, comfortable, and safe. I don't want or need a fancy new car. Money can't always buy happiness, but it can always help other people. Some people make a lot of money and spend it all on themselves. Some of the finer things in life don't impress me. But I will say I gained a love for flying my own aircraft. I've purchased a number of planes and helicopters over the years, which turned out to be a great benefit to my business and also a valuable resource to help people and share with others.

My first experience on a private plane came when Pat and I were coming back from Europe, and Wayne Valley offered to pick us up in New York. When the company became public—and more national—two years after I came on board, he decided to buy a Hawker 400 for the company to travel to cities around the country. We had annual meetings in Phoenix, Denver, and Mobile, Alabama. That day in New York, it was snowing and colder than heck. My wife was a little scared, but we took him up on the offer. We landed once to refuel and got dropped off in Oakland because Wayne was in nearby Piedmont. We'd go to different meetings on the plane. Naturally, I enjoyed it. That's how I got interested in flying privately.

I want to tell you about Jim Pandolfi, an architect who did work for us. We got to know each other pretty well. We were building small, affordable homes at the time, and he was clever with his plans. He suggested buying a piece of property in Santa Cruz with his doctor friend. I usually didn't do that sort of partnering, but I agreed, and Jim designed the building. Fast-forward to the late 1970s, when Jim took his wife, Inez, and daughter on a trip to Mexico. He was very adventurous and drove roads in the backcountry. Well, he got in a terrific accident, a head-on collision with a bus on a blind curve. He was given up for dead. We got a message from his doctor. If they didn't get him to a hospital, he would most likely die. Wayne Valley at the time had a small company plane, so I had to get his approval to use it. I said, "Wayne, we've got to get him out of there."

We contacted two pilots, and the doctor volunteered to go and took an assistant. I didn't go. There was limited space, a six-seater, and they had to take seats out to fit everyone. So it was two pilots, two medical people, and Jim, Inez, and their daughter, who were to be taken out on the plane.

At first they couldn't take Jim out of Mexico. He was being blamed for the accident and was going to be put in jail if he lived. It was a real problem. He was in bad shape. The doctor suggested possible brain damage. Inez and their daughter weren't as bad. Well, they ended up paying their way out of Mexico. Cash is king down there. They flew him back to Dominican Hospital in Santa Cruz and saved his life. I remember that like it was yesterday. If we hadn't had access to that plane, he would have died in Mexico, no doubt about it.

I always said to myself, "Once I get a little bit of money, I'm going to own a plane and fly myself." For the privacy and easy access to places.

An opportunity eventually came up. I became pretty tight with Jerry Levy, who was a character and worked for Lindsey Mortgage handling our mortgages. I flew on his plane a couple of times, a Hawker 400. I was in Philadelphia once to attend a 49ers game, and Jerry asked me to come over to Atlantic City for a night. I went over and gambled lightly, and he gambled big time. As it turned out, he was a big gambler and got in trouble with casinos, owing them a lot of money. He used the collateral from mortgages that weren't his and borrowed them to use for gambling.

Through Jerry, I met Jimmy the Greek, the legendary bookmaker, at the Kentucky Derby. My wife and I had dinner with Jerry and Jimmy, a great storyteller who was just like the person you saw on TV. He was a close friend of Al Davis, someone I did not have pleasant thoughts about because of the Wayne Valley stories, but Jimmy couldn't say enough good things about Al. Turns out, Jimmy's son was sick, and Al got a jet to pick up the son to fly him to one of the top children's hospitals and never charged him a dime for it.

Anyway, I ended up buying a plane from Jerry. Like a dummy. When you buy a plane, you're supposed to have it all checked out. He said he had done that. I didn't get an inspection. It flew fine. But when I went to sell it, it had a lot of issues, and I had to spend a lot of money on it. I learned my lesson. I flew it for a couple of years and felt I outgrew it.

I bought a Hawker 700 from British Air, almost brand-new. They overhauled it for me. I graduated to a Gulfstream III, a whole different plane and much bigger. It was capable of going from the Bay Area to Europe, and I had it for about four or five years. Then a Gulfstream IV-SP for another five years when I owned the A's. I used it for business but also baseball owners' meetings and games on the road. It was built custom, and I was fortunate to sell it for $4 million more than the purchase price. Amazing. That was the market.

Pat and I flew our plane to Europe at least once a year, and in 2001, we were in Prague, at our hotel, when we learned about the 9/11 terrorist attacks in New York. Such a depressing time, and we were just dumbfounded. We had just come in from Berlin, and we decided to try to come home if we could. But all flights coming in and out were shut down. The borders were closed, so we thought about flying into Canada, where I knew Gary Kirk and other friends, to wait.

"The patrons and employees at the hotel were so kind, expressing their sorrow and saying they were so sad to hear what happened in our country. We called our kids and watched the unbearable at the hotel all night. We were anxious to get home and be with our family, but all planes were grounded worldwide for five days. The pilots moved our plane to an American air base in Cologne. We drove to Cologne to get the plane, which had been camouflaged because it was a target with the American flag on the tail. Finally, after seven days, we got the go-ahead to leave. We thought we would fly to Canada and drive home, but as we were over the ocean, we got permission to fly to San Jose. We were the second private aircraft to land in our country, and we were so glad to be home.

"We had left New York for Europe three days before September 11. Our last view as we headed to Germany was of the World Trade Center. I remember that view so clearly. A few weeks later, we played the Yankees in the playoffs, and we were offered an escort to Ground Zero. Steve didn't want to go, so I went with our son. The crucifix standing, the smell, the silence, the chaos. I will never forget."

—Pat Schott

Chapter 40

Rush Limbaugh
and Paul Allen

WHILE HOUSE PRICES ARE supposed to go up, plane prices are supposed to go down. They're not supposed to hold value. You're not supposed to make money on planes, but I got lucky a few times. That's blind luck. Or great timing.

One was with Rush Limbaugh. Before that, I bought and sold planes but never made big money off the sales. This was different. Keith Simon, the 49ers' financial officer under Eddie DeBartolo, lost his job in the ownership changeover, and I hired him. He made a contact with a broker dealing with Rush Limbaugh, and I told Keith if we got this Limbaugh deal done with a Gulfstream 550, I'd give him a nice bonus, a finder's fee. I never forgot Keith. There was a deal on paper, and it was in escrow, but Limbaugh's attorneys were messing around with it. I was sweating it out.

I was in Indian Wells when I heard from friends at the Vintage Club that Limbaugh was a guest speaker at a party next door, and I went over there. It was good timing. I wanted to make sure he wasn't going to hold me up on this deal. I wouldn't have gone otherwise. He had a lot of listeners on the airwaves, but I didn't listen to him. He was kind of an arrogant guy. Anyway, the room was filled, 150 people with 10 tables. There was a little break, and I went over and sat down next to Limbaugh. He didn't know who I was. I talked with him about his early days working in the Kansas City Royals' clubhouse. I told him I was about to buy the A's. I also told him, "I'm the guy who's going to sell you the G550, but if you don't sign the contract, I've got to move on with somebody else because your attorneys are changing the whole deal around."

Limbaugh said he wanted the plane in the worst way and that he'd tell his attorneys to back off. There was a long waiting list, and he wanted one right away. One stipulation was that the plane had to be outfitted to satisfy his hearing loss, so the plane was engineered with that in mind. We got the deal done by the end of the week and closed on it two weeks later. He wanted it so badly that he paid $16.5 million over my price.

"When I was vice president of business operations and CFO of the 49ers, I remember recommending Steve take a look at buying the Tampa Bay Buccaneers. He had considered land-development deals in Florida, but that went by the wayside. After that, we became friends. Steve called and asked if I could help with financial stuff. I managed his helicopter company, helped him when he built a baseball stadium at Santa Clara University, and did a little work with the A's trying to find solutions. I think Steve liked that I was able to help with a lot of projects, and I did a lot of off-the-wall jobs that were really fun."

—Keith Simon

There was a similar story with Paul Allen, the Microsoft partner who owned the Seattle Seahawks at the time. I was buying a Gulfstream

650, and he wanted it right away. It was all about supply and demand and timing. Like with the Limbaugh plane, I had an option on it and was able to sell to Allen and make a significant profit because he was willing to pay $10 million more than my cost. The company eventually did away with that option buying. They knew how much I paid for it and realized they were losing money on these deals. I think eventually they referred to it as the Steve Schott Rule.

I don't have my own plane now. I fly in planes similar to how a condo time-share works. You buy hours. It turns out to be more expensive than owning your own plane, but it's less of a headache. It's always ready to go, and I don't have to service it. You see them used all the time by golfers. The money made in the sales to Rush Limbaugh and Paul Allen helps fund my flights today.

The helicopters I used were from Agusta, an Italian manufacturer. I remember I got a ride in Ken Hofmann's helicopter when we owned the A's, and I thought, "Boy, this is the way to go." But I didn't feel safe in his helicopter. I thought it was so small. So when I got a helicopter, it had two engines and two pilots. If one pilot couldn't fly for whatever reason, we had another. If one engine went out, we had another. We founded South Bay Helicopter, a company that has been available for executives to conduct business or anyone to tour the Bay Area and beyond, and ran it for 20 years before selling it in 2017.

"In the A's heyday, it was a blast. Running people around for meetings, picking up city council guys from Oakland, looking at stadium sites. It was fun to be part of. The big advantage over a plane is you're flying low and getting to sightsee the whole way. Instead of flying at 35,000 feet, you're at 700 to 1,000 feet, so you're seeing everything. We used the helicopter as a commercial charter service, to fly NASCAR people including Jeff Gordon, Roger Penske, and Rick Hendrick. We had Prince William

and Princess Kate. Bill Clinton, with his secret service, and he was in the back doing sudoku puzzles. Mick Jagger. A sundry list of movie stars. Tom Cruise, who's probably one of the nicest guys from Hollywood I've ever flown. He'd get out, walk around the helicopter, shake my hand, and say, 'Thanks, Mike.' The helicopter appeared in the original Avengers *movie—it crashes right at the beginning, though they used a prop helicopter for that. Cradle 2 the Grave. Bee Season with Richard Gere. The T-Mobile commercial with the girl getting off her motorcycle, jumping in the helicopter, which was colored pink, and turning the towns pink as she passed. But more than anything, it was a business tool. Steve's a consummate business guy. But when we started, Steve said he could afford to lose money but couldn't afford to be in the news. 'We can't have an accident.' So we turned down a lot of stuff if it was too much risk. I had so much fun with Steve and Pat as well. She's hilarious. There would be laughs and great conversations. I was like one of their kids, the kid in charge of their expensive toy."*

—Mike Phillips, helicopter pilot

Six people could be seated beside the pilots. We took it on vacation to Tahoe and to golf tournaments in Monterey and Napa, but it was also the perfect vehicle to scout properties. It was wonderful to work part of the day in the South Bay and get to the A's game by helicopter in the afternoon or night in Oakland, either land at the private terminal at the airport or, when there was room, the Coliseum parking lot.

Chapter 41

Golf Stories

ON THE GOLF COURSE, I'M A HACKER. I didn't take it too seriously. I shot in the 70s a couple times. That was pure luck. Everything was clicking, and I thought I had this game down. Next time out, I shot in the 90s. That's my usual score, high 90s or 100. I was a 19 or 20 handicap.

A long while back, I took lessons from Bob McGrath, the pro at San Jose Municipal Golf Course, a neat guy and great teacher. I was joining country clubs and wanted to learn more about the game. I did belong to the Los Altos Country Club and had an old set of clubs. A friend, Mike Rawitser, who operated golf courses, said I should upgrade my irons and woods and take lessons, and he pointed me to Bob McGrath. I figured I could just pick up the game. Of course, it's not that easy. I had never taken golf lessons. I never even had pitching lessons when I was a young ballplayer. These were my first, and I think they helped a little.

Well, Bob tried out for the 2007 PGA Championship and qualified as one of 20 club pros to play at Southern Hills in Tulsa. He was so excited, but there was an issue getting to Tulsa with his family. It was such a big deal and not something you could pass up. I wanted to do something for him, so I offered my plane to his family so they could fly to Tulsa and back. The Gulfstream IV-SP that seated 12. It was theirs to do with what they wanted, transportation to the big event. Boy, they were so excited. His mother, sister, and wife sent thank-you cards saying it was something they'd never forget and quoted something Bob said: "Life is about memories."

"I'm a club pro. I never dreamed of playing on tour. I was more of a baseball player like Steve was. I didn't play golf in college. I played one year in high school. And to have it fall on my lap at 50? This is for guys in their 30s. I had my game on to qualify at Sunriver Resort in Oregon, where I competed among 350 club pros. The San Jose Mercury *did a story on it, and I was quoted saying, 'Now I have to figure out how to get my whole family to Tulsa.' I got a call from Steve the next day, and he said, 'I think I could help you. Why don't you take my plane?' Are you kidding me? So yeah, all 10 of us got on the plane and flew to Tulsa.*

"Of course, Steve's plane was one of the best that came in. They were telling me Phil Mickelson's plane wasn't as nice. We received the royal treatment as if I were Tiger Woods or Phil Mickelson. It was a great opportunity for a lonely club pro from San Jose Muni to get treated like a tour pro for a week with all the legends around you. You go from the clubhouse to the range, and you'd hear, 'Player coming through,' like the sea was being parted for Moses. I'm not used to that kind of treatment. I got interviewed by the legendary columnist Art Spander, and I never ever expected that.

"Tiger won it, his 13th major title. One of the days, I was on 1 and he was on 4. My tee shot went into the rough of the fourth fairway, and here comes Tiger walking down the fairway, and my caddy and I waited for him to go through before I could take my second shot. I just wanted to get out of there. I couldn't see the green. I asked my caddy how far it was. He just looked at me. I wound up hitting a 5 iron to the green and got a little mini Tiger roar from the big crowd of people following him, so maybe I got a little sense of what he goes through. I actually parred the

hole. I shot an 80 and 78 the first two days, beat just a few guys, and tied Bubba Watson. The extravaganza of a PGA major was overwhelming and incredible. I felt like Jim Morris in the movie The Rookie, *the high school coach who pitches in the majors. This wasn't supposed to happen to me. I was supposed to be back at my desk in San Jose. I have a license plate frame, 'It's all about the memories,' and with Steve's help, these memories are phenomenal. I'll never forget them."*

—Bob McGrath, San Jose Municipal Golf Course golf pro

I have a lot of wonderful memories on the golf course. Playing with people I met in and out of business. I played in several pro-ams, including the Bob Hope Desert Classic, and a lot with George Graziadio, who cofounded Imperial Bank when he was young. The bank grew and grew, and I got to know him down in the desert through mutual friends and was on the board at the bank. He got to know Yogi Berra and would bring Yogi out to play with us. I was fortunate to play in the Tournament of Champions in Hawaii and Jerry Ford Invitational in Vail, Colorado. I'd play two days and never make the cut.

I once was in a foursome with the pro Steve Stricker, a genuinely nice and funny guy who hadn't made a name for himself yet. I was duffing the ball all over the place, and he had patience with me. I really enjoyed that. He went on to win 12 tournaments on the PGA Tour and captained the U.S. to the 2021 Ryder Cup championship. I never could have imagined him doing so well. Good things happen to nice guys. It also was a treat playing with Nick Faldo, one of the top players in history and former captain of the European Ryder Cup Team. He was so fun and easy to play with. I didn't have a caddy that day, and on one hole, I said, "Hey, Nick, could you size this putt up for par?" I was 17 to 20 feet from the hole. He said, "I see a break a little to the left; you've got to hit it firm." I sank the putt and joked to Nick, "You should've been my caddy all day." He laughed. What a good guy to be around.

Then there's the story of the Geibergers, father and son. Al Geiberger won 11 PGA tourneys in the 1960s and 1970s including the 1966 PGA Championship, but he might be best remembered for shooting a 59 in the 1977 Danny Thomas Memphis Classic—the first golfer in history to break 60 on the PGA Tour. Others have matched his 59, but he was the first. Well, years later, Al's son, Brent, caddied for me at Vintage Club. It was a summer job for Brent during college. Next thing I knew, he was on the PGA Tour himself, and I was chosen for his pro-am foursome in the Bob Hope Desert Classic. He was surprised to see me, as I was him, and gave me some of his personalized golf balls. Brent won a couple of PGA titles including the Chrysler Classic of Greensboro in 2004—the same tourney his dad won in 1976.

At the Vintage Club in 1996, I had a big thrill when I played with President Gerald Ford and sat at dinner with him and George. The three of us, just a fun round. President Ford was very anxious to play there. He was a hacker like the rest of us, but he was a good football player, I know that. At one point, I told him, "You're a great guy, but you could have hit them just a little bit more to the right." Not his politics but his golf game. He was hitting everything to the left. I was kidding, of course. He was as nice a man as you could ever find, as normal as could be. Nothing precocious about him, just very pleasant to be around and easy to talk to. Later, my wife, Pat, and I had dinner with the president, and he wrote me a letter dated February 23, 1996:

Dear Stephen:

I thoroughly enjoyed our golf game at Vintage and hope we can do it again. I'm correcting my wayward shots to the right, but holding steady philosophically.

Please come to Grand Rapids, Michigan, and see your Whitecap team in action where they average 7,000 per game and over 505,000 for the season.

If I get to Scottsdale during spring training I will let you know.

Warmest best wishes,

Gerald Ford.

We put on a lot of charity golf tournaments with the A's in Napa, and I must say, Mark McGwire could really whack a golf ball. One time we played together, I remember a par-4, about 300 yards, and he hit it all the way to the green. I told him he'd probably enjoy playing at Vintage Club, and he wanted to come down and play, but it never worked out. Mark Mulder was the best golfer on the team. After he was done playing, he won the Celebrity Golf Championship in Tahoe several years in a row. He was in the same charity event in Napa, playing in a foursome just ahead of McGwire and me. Right before McGwire hit the ball 300 yards, Mulder did the same. He yelled, "Watch this one, Schott" and hit it right on the green. I couldn't believe it.

We ran the golf tournaments every year and raised all kinds of money for our Read to Succeed program, which encouraged elementary school kids to read more. We later had our own tournament at my business, Citation Homes, also to raise money that helped kids get into reading.

"Steve was a big part of something beyond anything anyone could dream of. How can you say thanks? I sent him a shirt and hat from the Tulsa tournament. That seemed way short. I can't buy anything for him that could possibly show my thanks. My appreciation for what he did is beyond anything I could possibly come up with. It meant so much to me and all my family. Maybe my thankfulness can be conveyed through my words in this book."

—Bob McGrath

Chapter 42

10 Business Tips

I NEVER WAS TIMID about making a business decision, no matter how big or small. You don't want to dwell on something too long because you could change your mind a dozen times, so realize what's right and go with it. That's true for people breaking into a business or people already established. You've got to have certain rules to follow, otherwise it's helter-skelter. There are some pointers in business I like to fall back on, and here are 10 of them:

Surround Yourself with Successful People: This is so important. Meeting and working with people who can bring the most out of you and allow you to earn opportunities is essential and makes a huge difference. That remains true throughout life. Not just as someone working his way up but as a leader of a company. It still applies. When you're young, you learn from smart and successful people. Later, you hire the best and smartest people you anticipate will be successful.

Don't Be Overconfident: You can never know for sure if you've got the right answer. Or right solution. Or right decision. But have enough confidence in your decision-making or you're vacillating forever. It'll be harder to make a decision the longer you dwell on it. Weigh all the options, the pluses and minuses, and decide. You can't go one way because you have 10 positives and 5 negatives. That doesn't work. Because one negative could outweigh all the positives, and vice versa. They don't all weigh the same. Just look at the thing and ask, "Does it make sense based on how much money I have to put up?"

Don't Be Reckless: I definitely made mistakes. I was reckless. That comes from jumping to conclusions too quickly. People will ask, "How often are you right, 50-50?" You've got to be right more times than not or your business will go under. You'd like to be right at least 80 percent of the time while knowing that some bad decisions can ruin you.

Fly under the Radar: That's my whole general demeanor, and it takes me right back to baseball. If you're one of those guys who wants to let everyone know how great you are, how wealthy you are, you'll have a lot of pitfalls. Sometimes the less they know about you, the better.

Listen to Advice from Those Who Know: If someone's telling you a story about history, especially someone successful in life, listen. It could be about business. It could be about baseball. Anything. I was fortunate to spend a lot of time with Wayne Valley and Jack Brooks, who were partners in land development. It was an education being around them and soaking up their knowledge.

Find a Formula for Success and Stick to It: This is easier said than done because there's no definitive formula, but there are basics you could follow. For example, in homebuilding, one formula is to make sure you don't buy property before obtaining the entitlements that give you approval to build. Even today, after all these years, I haven't always followed the formula. We spent millions on a big piece of property that we shouldn't have bought until we had entitlements. I always preached not to do something like this, and we did. Five years later, we still haven't moved on it. It is a great property, too good to pass up, right in the heart of town. We had a plan we thought everyone would like, but there's resistance from people challenging the development, the NIMBYs—the not-in-my-backyard folks—who will tell you they're OK with development so long as it's not nearby. But this is not in a remote area. Boy, if you don't follow this rule, you can get your tail burned. I continue to learn by experience.

Don't Be a Know-It-All: I was never an outspoken guy. I never tried to put myself out there as a big shot. I learned a lot by working a lot of ground-floor jobs and never boasted or bragged while moving up. It does nothing but stroke the ego and doesn't accomplish anything.

Check and Recheck Your Facts: Do your homework. This goes for any business. In the case of homebuilding, do a market study before you decide what you'll build, even before you own the property. The type of house, attached or detached, large or small. There are six components for a homebuilder: sales, marketing, land acquisition, land development, finance/accounting, and construction. On all levels, know exactly what you're getting into, all your costs, and your competition. Don't leave anything out.

Borrow Frugally: Go with two banks, go with three. I like banks to be chasing me, not for me to be chasing banks. Find the cheapest rate. It's hard to make deals without money, without partners. On the other hand, there's no point in borrowing money if it's unnecessary. You're told you can't make money unless you have money. It's like the chicken or the egg. But I didn't always have money. I waited a long time to get my hands on money, and I remember at one point mortgaging my house for collateral.

Avoid Pitfalls: Once you make it, don't blow it. Don't do things you shouldn't be doing if there's no money to back you up, because you could lose it all. I've seen young guys make a few bucks and then go out and blow it because they act like multimillionaires and get crazy and buy fancy new cars and live the high life. I could have done it that way, but I'm not that type. One thing about Wayne Valley, he held much of our money and had it accrued so we wouldn't blow it. He wanted to make sure I didn't make a few bucks and then hit the road. Not that I haven't blown money in my life. I once put a million dollars in one stock, and it went up three or four times. When the dot-com boom crashed, that stock nosedived. I let it ride out all the way down to nothing. I can't have regrets. They don't help. Now, that sort of thing can happen in the stock market. I don't see it happening as much in real estate because there will always be residual value.

Part Seven

PRIDE IN THE ALMA MATER

Chapter 43

The Class of 1960

WE HAD A MOST UNUSUAL GRADUATING CLASS in 1960 at Santa Clara University. A lot of interesting and heroic people and personalities, including Leon Panetta—who served as presidential chief of staff, secretary of defense, and CIA director—and Everett Alvarez Jr., the first U.S. fighter pilot shot down over Vietnam and a prisoner of war in Hanoi for more than eight years.

Beyond Leon and Everett, it's a long list of many success stories about graduates who did big things in law, business, and many other fields. Maybe it was unique just by accident, but a lot of people did a lot of amazing things after graduation.

John Sobrato, another member of the class of 1960, was always working. We also went to Bellarmine together, and he was even working back then. John wasn't into sports. Sports was the main thing for me that got my juices flowing. While I was worried about chasing baseballs, John was out making money and preparing for his future. He received a real estate license as soon as he could and was selling houses when he wasn't at school. He was pretty focused and incentivized and drove fancy cars, I guess because of the real estate commissions.

Long Schott

John started at Santa Clara in engineering but found it was pretty time-consuming and switched to business. Well, he did very well for himself and became one of the biggest commercial developers through the Sobrato Organization and a multibillionaire who appears on the Forbes 400 list. We both went into developing, but I don't see it as a competition. He has developed a lot of commercial properties, apartments, and office buildings throughout the Silicon Valley.

"I really didn't make a lot of friends in my junior and senior years because I was working. Matter of fact, my picture is not in the yearbook my junior year because I wasn't there when they were taking photos. I was working. So I really didn't get to know Steve well until I became active on the boards at Santa Clara in the late '70s and early '80s. There wasn't a competition between us, none whatsoever. It was more of an admiration society. He did well at Citation Homes, and he probably thought I did well running Sobrato Development Companies. I just admire Steve's business career and actually what he was able to do with the A's without much money. He had the highest winning percentage in their history? Not surprising. He ran it like a business."
—John Sobrato

It's important to mention how generous John and his wife, Susan, have been as philanthropists supporting so many great causes, including giving many millions to the university and funding several buildings.

"John has given a lot to that campus. We served on the board of trustees together. I think with Santa Clara, there's a little symbol of the mission in his heart someplace. Likewise, Steve donated to many buildings, including the athletic building, Schott baseball field, and admission/enrollment building. They're both successful businessmen. God blessed them to have that ability to succeed in business, and to their credit, both of them have been very

generous with what they earned, not just to Santa Clara but to many other worthy causes as well. You could label them, in many ways, founding fathers of the modern Santa Clara campus, that's for damn sure."

—Leon Panetta

Father Paul Locatelli, also in our class, dedicated much of his life to Santa Clara, including two decades as president of the school when it grew to the flourishing university it is now. He had the vision and headed fundraising, and people felt good donating to the school knowing he was the point man. He would seal the deal, and it was as if people thought they were giving both to the university and Paul Locatelli. He increased the endowment from $77 million to $700 million due to good investments, and upgraded the academic buildings and sports facilities. He was not a sports guy but did a lot for women's sports. The football program ended on his watch, but I can't blame him for that. It wasn't going anywhere, and it was expensive. They were in a lower division and couldn't draw much revenue. He pushed to drop it, but at the time, a lot of smaller football programs at colleges were being dropped.

I met Paul when we were both in accounting at Santa Clara. We weren't close friends. He was more serious than I was and didn't follow sports much at all. I lost track of him after graduating, but I bumped into him when we were in the Army Reserve together. Then he found his calling. I always kidded with him, "You couldn't take the Reserve, so you joined the seminary." The next thing you know, he was ordained, a priest and university president.

Paul died at 71 in 2010, shortly before our 50-year reunion, and when I committed $1 million for a new Palo Alto Medical Facility medical building, my doctor, Bart Lally, who cared for Paul in his final days, asked me if my name would be on the building, and I deferred to Paul. It's called the Paul L. Locatelli Center for Cancer Care. For many, he's remembered as a fellow student, priest, professor, dean of the business school, academic vice president, president chancellor, and wonderful leader and friend.

> *"You wonder if there was something in the water with that class—a class of about 250 men, one of the last all-male classes at Santa Clara. To think of the impact they had on the university is just amazing, unlike any class before or since. Having Father Paul in the class was a big thing. When he was president and looking to engage people, he turned to his amazing friends first. They've had a real sense of commitment to each other and the university."*
>
> **—Mike Wallace, assistant vice president of development at Santa Clara and liaison for alumni**

We had a bunch of good athletes in our class, and two of the best were Frank Sobrero, a standout basketball player who was a leading scorer and made All-WCC, and Jim Derry, the quarterback on the football team, who lived a block down from John Sobrato in Atherton and later was close with the former 49ers quarterback John Brodie; they played cards together. Jim was a very radical guy but good athletic talent.

A long while back, Santa Clara had a very powerful football program and played in three major bowl games, winning them all: the Sugar Bowl in 1937 and 1938, when Santa Clara was coached by Buck Shaw, and the 1950 Orange Bowl, when Len Casanova was the coach and Santa Clara beat Kentucky and the legendary Bear Bryant. The school dropped major college football a couple of years later for financial reasons but brought it back in 1959, and that's when Jim Derry became quarterback. There were no scholarships right away, and Jim wasn't a high school quarterback, but he was such a good athlete that he came along and became a very good college quarterback. Later, quarterback Dan Pastorini and tight end Brent Jones were drafted out of Santa Clara, but the school folded the program again in 1992, saying it got too expensive and didn't fit in the budget.

It was a tremendous class, 1960. Leon, Everett, John, Paul, and many others. Dick Creighton, my teammate who pitched on the school's baseball team with me. Tom Hastings, my friend and a superior court judge—we were together in grammar school, high school, and college. Butch Erbst, the point man for our class, who has done terrific work keeping us all together. Lou Castruccio, a renowned tax attorney in Los Angeles who serves on Santa Clara's board of trustees. And many more people with great stories to tell. I'm proud of the people in our class and all they've accomplished.

Chapter 44

Leon Panetta, an American Success Story

LEON PANETTA WAS AND IS A VERY LIKABLE and personable guy, and it's an honor to say Leon was part of our class of 1960. He was a dorm guy—a dormer, as we used to say. We were casual acquaintances, and I got to know him a lot better in later years.

Leon did so much good for the country. For the most part, no one had a bone to pick with him, including as a politician, first as a Republican and later as a Democrat and California congressman. I'm a Republican, and I support him still. He was a military intelligence officer in the Army, and politically he is respected on both sides of the aisle.

"Steve's a good American who really cares about his country. We were in a class that bonded at the time for a lot of reasons. One was because we had some great personalities in the class who reached out and were friendly.

"In my political career, I've attributed a lot to the Jesuits teaching me to have a conscience about right and wrong. That guidance proved very helpful in politics. In politics and,

with Steve, in the business world, you can be tempted to do a lot of things, and having that sense of right and wrong was invaluable in making sure you do the right thing. Everything I've done in politics, the success is based on the human touch. If somebody can relate to others and understand others, you can make things happen. That's the nature of politics and the nature of Washington, and it was the nature of Santa Clara in our class. A lot of us were able to relate to one another, build bonds of friendship. We were an all-male school, and going to the pizza parlor and ordering some pitchers of beer—maybe more than a few pitchers of beer—was the thing to do, and Steve was very much a part of that. There was a lot of spirit on campus and good support for athletics. The basketball team was very good, and for baseball games, we didn't hesitate to grab a few beers and sit in the stands because it was usually a warm day.

"I remember Steve as obviously one of the better players, a pitcher along with Dick Creighton. But I've got to tell you, Steve was a hell of a hitter. I remember him being able to connect. Maybe it was more a fact he was a tall guy and just looked intimidating when he got up to the plate."

—Leon Panetta

At Santa Clara, Leon was involved with student leadership and graduated magna cum laude with a political science degree. He returned for a doctorate in law, taught a political science course, gave commencement speeches, and served on the board of trustees for two decades. A true proponent of the university.

"When I was student body officer, we had open houses around the first part of the school year, and we'd invite all the Catholic women's schools. It was probably a conspiracy by the nuns and priests; at least my wife is convinced that was the case. The women bused in, and we'd greet them and put a corsage on them as they came off the bus. It was our way of being nice

Catholic boys but also a way to check out the women as they were getting off the bus.

"I wasn't planning on attending the mixer, and Butch Erbst came in my room and said, 'No, no, let's go to the mixer.' What the hell? So I came charging out of our dorm, and there was a group of women walking by, one of whom was named Sylvia, who was attending Dominican College in San Rafael at the time, and I had remembered her coming off the bus. I hooked up with her, and after the dance, I walked her back to the bus. Sylvia and I have been married for 60 years. I owe a lot to Santa Clara."

—Leon Panetta

Politically, Leon tried to bring subjects to light in the right way, tried to bring people together while serving in many positions over the years under both Republican and Democratic presidents. Leon was a champion for civil rights and balanced budgets, and he helped preserve the California coast.

I'm proud to say he oversaw the operation that took down Osama bin Laden, who was killed as part of a mission by U.S. Navy SEALS on May 2, 2011. Leon was CIA director at the time, and the mission ended a 10-year manhunt for the world's most wanted terrorist and leader of al-Qaeda who was responsible for the murder of 3,000 Americans on September 11, 2001. Three previous CIA directors tried to gather intelligence to take down bin Laden, and that was a key objective of Leon's when he took over the CIA in 2009. As President Obama revealed immediately after the mission, "Shortly after taking office, I directed Leon Panetta, the director of the CIA, to make the killing or capture of bin Laden the top priority of our war against al-Qaeda." Leon brought urgency to the pursuit, and when the day came, he moved forward with the operation on orders from the president. Bin Laden was killed at his compound in Pakistan, his body buried at sea.

"That was a proud moment. The ability to put the intelligence together to be able to track him and find where he was and work with special forces and do the operation, I've got to tell you, it was a very special memory mainly because it was really the best of America coming together to deliver justice to people who died on 9/11. I've never forgotten that."

—Leon Panetta

After leaving Washington, Leon founded the Panetta Institute for Public Policy, a nonpartisan, nonprofit study center to which I donate every year. It does a lot of good, including recruiting students with different backgrounds into public service and preparing them for such a life. That he was confirmed by the Senate in a rare vote of 100–0 as President Obama's secretary of defense shows how he was universally respected.

"It's about love of country. Which isn't partisan and shouldn't be partisan. It's about doing what's in the best interest of the country. That's what should motivate people who get into politics, and for that matter all of us."

—Leon Panetta

Chapter 45

Everett Alvarez Jr., an American Hero

ONE OF MY PEERS IN THE CLASS OF 1960 is a true American hero whose story needs to be known by everyone.

Everett Alvarez Jr. was the first U.S. fighter pilot shot down over Vietnam. He was a prisoner of war in Hanoi, in captivity for eight years and seven months—from August 5, 1964, to February 12, 1973, when he was released. He endured torture and beatings and experienced heinous things most of us can't imagine.

We knew Everett as a very nice guy, a smart guy from Salinas who earned an academic scholarship at Santa Clara. If you didn't live on campus, you were called day dogs. Most students lived on campus, the dormers, and they all had a connection with each other. Everett and I were day dogs, and I'd occasionally see him in the library. He was an electrical engineering major, and I wasn't smart enough to hang out with those guys. I remember him being pretty quiet and not outgoing or aggressive at all. I couldn't have imagined him as a fighter pilot.

A few years after college, while many of the rest of us were thinking about our next dollar or meal, Everett was flying missions in the military. The day he was shot down, he was flying an A-4C Skyhawk as part of the Attack Squadron 144 from the carrier USS *Constellation*. The North Vietnamese kept him as a POW at the Hoa Lo Prison.

"For eight and a half years, my connection to Santa Clara was in memories, not of any particular individual but more of a community memory. Also my family. And close childhood friends. Such as Joe Kapp, who played football and basketball at Berkeley. We were both from Salinas.

"When I came back from Vietnam, coming to Santa Clara was like coming home. Father Walter Schmidt, a university vice president, and Jim Shea, a university trustee, were there for me and took me under their wings, always there to support me. Father Schmidt was a mentor, and I was very close with him. Jim Shea was a businessman and good friend. He had four sons and felt close to me—one of his sons, Jim Jr., was a Navy pilot killed in Vietnam. After graduation, I went straight into the military. When I came back, my name was out there, and I was involved in the school's activities over the years, which is how I got to know everyone else much better, including Steve. And of course Leon Panetta, who started getting involved in congressional politics. I got to know him more when he was in Congress and I was serving in the Reagan administration."

—Everett Alvarez Jr.

For his distinguished career and heroism, Everett is recognized in Salinas, where kids are getting educated at Everett Alvarez High School, and a park in Santa Clara is named in his honor (as are a post office in Maryland, a hangar at the Naval air station in Kingsville, Texas, and a housing project at the Naval air station in Lemoore, California). At Santa Clara University, Everett is a lifetime member of the board of fellows. The list of recognitions and accolades is long and all deserved. Under President Reagan, Everett was the deputy director of the Peace Corps and deputy administrator of the Veterans Administration.

> *"Everett, like John McCain, went through some tough times during the Vietnam War. When I became secretary of defense, I understood the sacrifice the men and women in uniform made to put their lives on the line in order to protect the country, and thank God we have brave people like Everett who were able to do that.*
>
> *"When I was in the Army from '64 to '66 and in Washington as a legislative assistant to U.S. Senator Tom Kuchel of California starting in '66, Everett was missing in action. It was only later we found out he was one of the POWs. At the time, the senate was obviously heavily debating the war in Vietnam. Everett not only was my classmate at Santa Clara but a hometown kid, from my home area in Salinas. We went to ROTC together. When he came back from Vietnam, it was amazing, and it was amazing that he survived. Everybody understood the sacrifice he made for this country."*
>
> —Leon Panetta

What a hero Everett is with the strength and perseverance he showed after getting shot down. I wanted to do something for him and set up a scholarship in his name at Santa Clara, which still is being funded. He was more deserving than anybody. I wanted to keep it anonymous, but somehow word got out.

> *"Steve set up a $1 million scholarship at Santa Clara in Everett's name but didn't want Everett to know. He somehow found out about it and thanked Steve. Mike Wallace at the university arranged for us to meet for coffee, and that's when Everett told Steve how much he appreciated it. Of course, we all appreciated what Everett did."*
>
> —Butch Erbst, class of 1960

When we got together at our 55-year reunion in 2015, and I got together with Everett and his wife, I just wanted him to know why I did it. He was very thankful for the tribute, and I'm happy I could do something like that for him.

"I told Steve, 'I thought it might've been you.' I wasn't sure. I just think so highly of him. In college, I knew who he was because of sports. He was in the student paper all the time as a well-known baseball player, and when I was in the library, I'd sometimes see this fellow across the way studying. When I came back from Vietnam, I got to know more about him because of Ed Alvarez, who's no relation, but Ed filled me in. He was also in our class at Santa Clara and was an attorney for the 49ers and later joined Steve and helped at Citation Homes and with the A's when Steve owned the team. The class of 1960, a number of people had done quite well with the development of the Silicon Valley and Santa Clara. In a way, I try to give back a little bit when I get a chance. As for the scholarship, I receive a briefing on it every year. It really helps some students coming through, and I'm glad it does. I'm very grateful for Steve doing that."

—Everett Alvarez Jr.

Part Eight

GIVING BACK

Chapter 46

A New Ballpark

WE NEVER HAD VERY GOOD FIELDS when I was in school. There was nothing special about the diamond at Bellarmine. Not much room for fans to sit and watch. It was right along the railroad tracks in San Jose—you knew when a freight or passenger train was pulling into the College Park stop. If we had a big game, we'd play at Washington Park, a little bandbox, the same field where I played my Pony League games. It was a short poke to right field, so they had to put up a high screen. Left-handed hitters could pop it over the fence pretty easily. Today, Bellarmine has a wonderful facility, and the field is named after Bob Fatjo, my old coach.

In college, we played in the same conference as USC, UCLA, Stanford, and Cal, a five-school league, and tried to hold our own athletically, but we were nowhere close with our facilities. As freshmen, we played at Ryan Field, which was more of a cow pasture, a wide-open hay field, a crappy field with a little diamond and an ROTC drill area on the far end. You heard of the Field of Dreams? This was the field of nightmares. The varsity played off campus at Washington Park, the field we used my final three years at Santa Clara through 1960, and the 1962 team that played in the College World Series championship game also played there. There were no wind barriers, so the wind would just howl through. I think it's a reason I hurt my arm out there.

Things changed in 1963 when the baseball team moved to Buck Shaw Stadium, which was built at Ryan Field and named after the first coach of the San Francisco 49ers. Buck Shaw played for Knute Rockne at Notre Dame, a lineman blocking for George Gipp. He also was a kicker—and coached at Santa Clara before running the 49ers from the mid-1940s to the mid-1950s. Buck Shaw Stadium wasn't really a ballpark. It was a facility where they played football and soccer, and it was converted into a baseball park for baseball season, which got expensive.

I always thought Santa Clara's baseball team should have its own facility, something far better than the fields I played on and something superior to Buck Shaw Stadium, which was built with funds raised by the Bronco Bench Foundation, a great organization that still assists the athletic department and funds scholarships. I talked to Father Paul Locatelli, the Santa Clara president who graduated with me in 1960, about building a singular baseball facility. One thing led to another, and we built a new state-of-the-art baseball home on the east part of campus. Finally, Santa Clara had a baseball-only facility. I put in $4 million, and they named it Stephen Schott Stadium. I felt honored to help get Santa Clara one of the nation's top college baseball complexes with 1,500 seats, a really nice upgrade. It's all there—home clubhouse, training facilities, batting cages, video systems, meeting room, press box, luxury suite.

"When it opened, it meant instant credibility for the baseball program. We became a player not just within the conference but the region. It elevated the profile of the program in terms of respect and recruiting and also being able to use that facility

to attract other events, to bring people to the campus and get exposure not only for the baseball program but for Santa Clara generally. There was no limit to Steve's generosity when it came to Santa Clara."

—Dan Coonan, president and CEO of the Eastern College Athletic Conference and former Santa Clara athletic director

Clay Wood, the outstanding groundskeeper with the A's, volunteered to help with the field and drainage. He's so good and came down several times to check on it. I knew there could be issues because it was all flat ground. I mentioned it to Clay, and he said he'd be happy to come down and check it out. He said, "You know what? This is what I live for." He's a terrific guy and did a great job. The field would not have withstood as much water if the drainage hadn't been set up right.

I think the best compliment I heard was from Tony Gwynn, the Hall of Famer and San Diego State coach who said this was one of the finest college ballparks he had been in. It was a pleasure that Tony brought his team to Santa Clara for nonconference games after the stadium opened, and I was very impressed someone like Tony would offer a compliment of that significance.

"At Buck Shaw, players would go in the mini locker room after games and get out as soon as they could. Once the new stadium was built, they wouldn't leave. They wanted to sleep over. It's a one-stop shop, unbelievable from a player-development and recruiting standpoint. When Tony's San Diego State team visited, I gave him a tour of the entire facility, and he said, 'This is one of the nicest facilities on the West Coast. I can't imagine a nicer facility.' That was after he said, 'This coaching thing is overrated. They're not listening to me.' I told him, 'If they're not listening to you, they're sure not listening to me.' Anyway, it never would've happened without Steve Schott. He's such a humble guy, and I

don't think he realizes the impact he made with former players and current players as well."
—Mark O'Brien, Santa Clara baseball coach, 2002–11

I love the Santa Clara stadium. Unfortunately, we didn't get a new ballpark for the A's in those years. At the time, we were looking at different areas, including a site in Santa Clara where Levi's Stadium was built, now the home of the 49ers. It would have been nice if building a stadium for the A's could have been as simple as building on a college campus. From talking with Father Locatelli to committing to the financial pledge in January 2004 to its opening in April 2005, it was a wonderful project, and they asked me to throw the ceremonial first pitch before the first game. I hadn't thrown a baseball in years; I was 66 at the time. Of course, I didn't warm up and bounced it to the plate. I should have walked halfway to the catcher's box.

Chapter 47

Dedicating an Athletic Center

HENRY SCHMIDT WAS A LONGTIME TIRELESS, famous athletic trainer who worked for the San Francisco 49ers, Los Angeles Rams, and Golden State Warriors and also was a regular at the East-West Shrine Game, which annually brings together the nation's top college football players.

Schmidty meant the world to me and countless other college kids because his main job for 50 years was working as the head trainer at Santa Clara University, from 1927 to 1977. He was always there for me. I had a lot of back tightness, and he'd work the knots out, rub me down before and after games, and get me ready to pitch throughout the season.

Santa Clara has built a beautiful new all-purpose athletic facility that I was proud to help fund and which will do so much for the students and the university, making it more possible for them to recruit some high-level athletes. The 50,000-square-foot facility is top-notch and usable by athletes from all the sports, and within the facility is a special room that was added, an auxiliary trainer's room named after Henry Schmidt, one of the best trainers in the world—a great tribute to a great man.

> *"The Stephen C. and Patricia A. Schott Athletic Excellence Center, in my mind, is the best college athletic facility in the conference and maybe the West Coast, and it's all because Steve believed in us and believed in Santa Clara athletics and gave us an incredibly generous gift to let us have this amazing building. When I got to Santa Clara six years ago, we didn't have a treadmill in our weight room. I'm forever thankful to Steve and Pat for giving us a chance to be highly competitive. Henry Schmidt is someone Steve thinks very highly of, and Steve was relentless, in a good way, by writing a lot of letters to recruit friends, alumni, and ex-teammates to contribute for the satellite trainer's room."*
>
> —Renee Baumgartner, Santa Clara athletic director

I got involved with the athletic excellence center because there was a need, and I wanted the university to reach its potential athletically. It started with a push from the men's basketball coach, Herb Sendek, who told me how badly they needed an all-purpose building. Herb came to Santa Clara with good credentials. His previous two coaching gigs were at North Carolina State and Arizona State, and when he was at N.C. State, coaching in the ACC, he advanced to the NCAA Tournament five straight years and earned the respect of Duke's legendary coach Mike Krzyzewski.

I know that because I ran into Coach K in Las Vegas. It was a brief, accidental meeting. My wife was gambling alongside Coach K and got to talking with him, and she introduced me to him. He was playing 50 dollars a hand. I prefer 10 dollars a hand. Anyway, I said, "Coach K, you don't know me, but Santa Clara just hired a guy I think you know,

Herb Sendek." He said, "Oh, great guy. You've got a good one there," a good compliment from Coach K.

I told Herb that. When he was hired, he wanted to meet me because I've been a basketball contributor more than any other sport, and my brother, Larry, loved basketball and was huge into fundraising for the program and funding scholarships. Herb told me about the need for a new building. Personally, I wanted to do something, and Renee came to me. We talked about a figure, and I agreed to donate with the stipulation that others would donate as well.

It worked out nicely. It has two stories, a sports performance center, academic center, sports medicine center, a fuel station, two practice gyms and, of course, the Schmidt auxiliary trainer's room, all so these kids could be in one dedicated place to train, eat, study, and just hang out.

"Steve donated $15 million. He wanted us to be really good in athletics, and we needed a lead gift. His donation was the single biggest game changer for what was accomplished. He wanted his donation to be matched within a year by other donors, and we did it. In fact, 81 percent of the cost was raised by former student-athletes, which is unheard of. I honestly believe they were moved by Steve being a former baseball player at Santa Clara. The other 19 percent came from other donors and fans. Aside from Steve and Pat, we received $10 million from Mary and Mark Stevens—Mary played soccer at Santa Clara, and Mark is in the Warriors' ownership group—and they were instrumental in funding our soccer facility, Stevens Stadium.

"Of course, our women's soccer team won the national championship in 2021, and a lot of players on that team came here knowing they'd be able to utilize our Schott Athletic Excellence Center. We were able to use it as a selling point for our recruits, and it's a dream come true. If we succeed, especially in men's basketball and baseball and women's volleyball and

soccer, it'll help with fundraising and bringing the community together, and Steve and Pat know how important that is for Santa Clara on the national stage."

—Renee Baumgartner

My name did not have to be attached to the building, but my name and Pat's name are up there. It's not why I did it. They told me they badly needed the funds to help recruiting with basketball and all the team sports. It needed a name. All the buildings on campus have names. I never wanted to be a guy with his name up in lights. I was never impressed with those guys, the flashy guys. I told myself if I ever made a lot of money, I wouldn't want to be that kind of guy. It's more than that. It's also about trying to be a decent person and help people who can use the money. In this case, it was about helping my alma mater get to the next level. From what they've told me, it's the greatest thing to hit the university and will greatly benefit student-athletes. The dedication was in September 2021, and I spoke off the cuff to a couple of hundred people, mostly students, about my life, career, and time at Santa Clara.

"I was the mayor of Santa Clara and had been to tons of dedications for buildings and statues and such things, but that was my favorite dedication because it was so personal. I was shocked when I heard Steve's speech. He's so humble, and I know he put his heart and soul into that building as he had done with others. In his speech, he sat and talked about his roots and how Santa Clara was important to him and gave the message, 'Don't give up, work hard, and you'll be successful.' It reminded me of—and I'm old enough to go back this far—the Fireside Chats from President Roosevelt. It was a beautiful occasion, and Steve was very impressed with the kids. The track team was there. The women's soccer team, which won the national title,

was there. Surrounded by the Santa Clara athletes, he told them after seeing all those kids that he felt what he did to make the athletic building possible was all worthwhile."

—Gary Gillmor, former Santa Clara mayor

I'm just glad Schmidty is recognized. Back when I played ball, we didn't have diddly in terms of a trainer's room. We had a hole in the wall—a couple of tables and a whirlpool. We didn't know any better. Now they've got an 8,000-square-foot state-of-the-art training facility, which includes the Henry Schmidt auxiliary trainer's room that's right off the Rambis Family Gymnasium, named after Kurt Rambis, who played basketball at Santa Clara before joining the Showtime Lakers in the 1980s.

Schmidty had an influence on so many athletes who went through Santa Clara. He was among the five founding members of the National Athletic Trainers Association in 1950 and is in the Athletic Trainers Association Hall of Fame. Somebody finally said, "This guy deserves some recognition. Why not name a room after him?" It wasn't me, it was John Micek from the class of 1974, but once I heard about it, I was all in and called a lot of athletes whom Schmidty took care of. We wanted to raise $100,000, so we put on a full-court press, and I reached out to former athletes to chip in. It was, "Hey, give 2,500 bucks and you can have your name on the plaque in front. He was such a hardworking guy and did so much for us, the least we can do is donate $2,500 or even $1,000 in his name." We raised more than $125,000. It was a nice grassroots effort. I was surprised with how many people stepped up.

It's interesting. Schmidty lived right around the corner from us. I knew the family pretty well before I attended Santa Clara. He had four kids, three boys—two of whom died tragically in automobile accidents: Henry Jr. and Billy, who was a very good athlete. He played baseball at

Santa Clara and was a quarterback at Bellarmine and continues to be honored at the high school, which gives out the Billy Schmidt Award to athletes for their exemplary conduct and leadership.

"In his field, my father was the best. He knew the body better than anybody. Everybody liked him. On his watch, the football team went to two Sugar Bowls and an Orange Bowl and won them all. I'm glad he's being honored, and I'm thankful for Steve. I remember Steve well, living right behind him. He's a go-getter, a good person, always a gentleman, and I appreciate his support.

"I remember I was a water boy working for my dad, and I still have the water wagon that they wheeled out there during a timeout. The school wanted to throw it away, so my dad brought it home. It's heavy and made of cast iron, still with a brass plaque saying it was presented by Edmund Lowe, a movie star who went to Santa Clara, and the class of 1910. It should be in a museum or back on campus.

"My dad was with the Rams when they went to the NFL Championship Game in 1950, and years later when I went in the service, I got a Rams tattoo on my arm. I said, 'Look, Dad.' He said, 'Silly ass. What did you do that for? I just went to work for the 49ers.'"

—Bob Schmidt, son of Henry Schmidt

Schmidty was ahead of his time, and he's still remembered by many. A park is named in his honor in the city of Santa Clara, Henry Schmidt Park, eight acres with lots of fields and courts for the public to enjoy. It opened when my friend Gary Gillmor was the Santa Clara mayor. His daughter, Lisa, is the mayor now and has had her share of sparring with the 49ers. The park includes a "wall of fame" displaying pictures from Schmidty's long career as a trainer and many famous athletes and not-so-famous athletes whom he helped.

Chapter 48

The Horatio Alger Award

MANY AMAZING PEOPLE HAVE WON the prestigious Horatio Alger Award, which generally is given to 10 to 12 Americans every year, and I'm honored to be included on the list after receiving the award in 2001.

It was a thrill when my family, friends, and I spent a few days in Washington, where that year's recipients were acknowledged at the White House by President George W. Bush. In front of a large crowd and a lot of dignitaries, he singled me out as "a managing partner of a baseball team—and I know how much he suffers," which got a lot of laughs because Bush had owned the Texas Rangers before I bought the A's.

The days in Washington, I'll never forget. We visited several important landmarks. Aside from the White House, they gave us a tour of the Supreme Court, where we had our reception and were introduced and honored. Clarence Thomas, the Supreme Court justice, gave us beautiful medallions. The final night, we were inducted into the association at a formal event and received our awards, and a short biographical video was shown for each of us. They had come out and taken video of me in my old neighborhood and grammar school. They had asked me about goals, and I said it's not necessarily important to set goals extremely high as much as continuing to raise the bar, and if you keep raising the bar, you could get the breaks you need. Once you get your break, it's up to you to deliver and keep pushing yourself. If you set a goal and accomplish that goal, then what do you do next? By raising the bar over and over, it means you've got to keep achieving something else. That's part of my philosophy. What do you do next? Well, you raise the bar and do something better.

They asked me to submit a quotation, and mine was, "I don't measure success in financial terms. It's how you lead your life and what you give back to the community." On that front, while I was thrilled to receive the award, there's more to it. It's about further committing to helping young people get educations through need-based college scholarship programs, which I'm doing now at Santa Clara, providing up to 12 scholarships a year. You're expected to be a Horatio Alger supporter throughout your life, and I've gladly partnered by giving upward of $3 million to the association. Speaking of which, a great thing about the Horatio Alger event in Washington was that young students were honored for their own success and overcoming adversity. Education is the key for these kids to pursue their dreams, and I'm trying to help provide them opportunities.

Horatio Alger was the distinguished author in the 1800s who focused on rags-to-riches stories, writing young adult novels about people who came from humble beginnings and worked hard, lived right, and overcame adversity to succeed in life. According to the association, the award symbolizes its "values, including personal initiative and perseverance, leadership and commitment to excellence, belief in the free-enterprise system and the importance of higher education, community service, and the vision and determination to achieve a better future."

Candidates can't be born into money. It's about rising from humble means and reaching success. They were very strict about that. Winners come from many walks of life, from the world of sports (Hank Aaron, Wayne Gretzky, Roger Staubach) to acting (Denzel Washington, Tom Selleck, James Earl Jones) to entertainment (Bob Hope, Carol Burnett, Danny Thomas) to music (Waylon Jennings, Quincy Jones, Johnny Cash) to politics (Herbert Hoover, Gerald Ford, Ronald Reagan). And a lot more. Some other recipients included astronaut Buzz Aldrin, Air Force general and test pilot Chuck Yeager, and journalist Tom Brokaw.

Also, a lot of businesspeople have been honored, such as my friend Dennis Washington, who briefly went to Bellarmine and has given a lot of money to the association. I have a lot of respect for Dennis, a classy person who has a wonderful story and got into construction like I did and developed one of the largest companies in the country, eventually getting into mining and the railroad. He's from Montana and has a place in Indian Wells, which I've visited, and has helped a lot of young people through his philanthropy.

"Steve is a classic Horatio Alger, coming from little means and believing in helping kids. It's the largest need-based program for providing scholarships for kids. We had kind of a parallel journey as far as where we started and going through life. People who become successful and don't give back and aren't philanthropic, they're not only cheating others they could help, but they're cheating themselves. One of the real rewards in life is giving back and enjoying the fruits you made to help others, and Steve certainly didn't cheat himself. He walked his talk, a humble and down-to-earth guy."
—Dennis Washington, founder of the Washington Companies

Dennis is a member of the Vintage Club in Indian Wells, and quite a few other members received the Horatio Alger Award as self-made people. One is Richard Knowlton, who was the one who nominated me. As a young kid, he got a job as a butcher at the Hormel Foods Corporation and worked his way up to become CEO, a fascinating story.

Going back to Washington for the award was a wonderful honor and opportunity, and I was fortunate to share it with my wife, three children, their spouses, and some friends. I went back to the event several times, which is encouraged. Considering the list of people inducted before me, I was extremely proud to be involved in this worthwhile venture and give back to a great cause.

Chapter 49

Honoring the Military

AT THE SUMMIT OF MOUNT UMUNHUM, situated in the Santa Cruz Mountains, just south of San Jose in Santa Clara County, with stunning views of the bay and the coastal range all the way into Monterey and Carmel, I worked on a survey crew as a kid.

This mountain has historic significance because an Air Force radar tower still stands on its peak and was used during the Cold War to search the skies for Soviet planes, an integral part of our early-warning defense system. This was back when it was a regular little village with homes, a community center, and military families living on the base, which was open from 1957 to 1980 and closed when satellites made it antiquated.

Ever since, they've been trying to figure out what to do with the 85-foot-high building atop the 3,500-foot mountain, a cube-shaped concrete structure that can be seen across the South Bay. There has been talk of demolition, and I've worked hard to keep them from tearing it down by contributing to preserving and restoring the structure. I think it's important for visitors to know what once was up there. In the 1950s, I did survey work up there while construction of the base was in progress, so I'm familiar with the history and would like others to know it as well.

At Santa Clara, we were required to enroll in the Reserve Officer Training Corps, ROTC, our freshman and sophomore years. I opted not to do it as a junior and senior so I could concentrate on baseball. Not long after graduating from college, I joined the Reserve. I did basic training at Fort Ord on Monterey Bay, spent six months in active duty at Fort Gordon in Georgia, and graduated as a military policeman, trained with M1 rifles and .45 caliber handguns. Four of those months involved active police duty, whether it was patrolling in town or at the post. Those six months seemed like six years. You're a kid with your life in front of you, but it was our way of serving our country. A lot of us joined the Reserve to avoid the draft. That's the way it was. We weren't draft dodgers, but we were taking the alternate route. A few years later, they ended the draft, but during my time, you didn't have a choice unless you got classified as 4-F and were deemed medically ineligible. A lot of guys ran to Canada. I knew some of them. That wasn't an option for me. We did our part.

The base was in Augusta, home of the Masters. At the time, I didn't know diddly about golf, but I was nearby when the tournament was played. In retrospect, I should have gone over there and watched Arnold Palmer and Jack Nicklaus, who were dominating that tournament back then, and all the other greats from the era.

I spent the next five and a half years in the Reserve, including in 1962 amid the Cuban Missile Crisis under President Kennedy when Khrushchev placed Soviet nuclear missiles on the island, 90 miles from Florida. It was an intense time and gripped the nation, and the guys in our unit thought we might get called. We were on alert, ready to go. I later got letters from two or three guys I knew from basic training who got called. We never did.

During the five and a half years in the Reserve, we served every other weekend with our unit in San Jose and spent two weeks every summer training at Camp Roberts in Central California, where we conducted war games to simulate the action, teach situational awareness, and prepare for combat scenarios. Inter-Service Intelligence is what you'd call it. I got married when I was 23, so I was married for four of those years and raising a family.

Those two weeks every summer in the Reserve were the only two weeks I got for vacation at Ford Motor Company and later a couple of relatively small building companies. I was making $600 a month without many benefits. So for much of the 1960s. I spent my vacation not by enjoying my family but living outside in tents and performing different drills at Camp Roberts.

I was never going to make the military a career. I feel I did my obligation. I received an honorable discharge, which they give when you finish your duty. It's clear why I have the attachment to the radar tower atop Mount Umunhum, named after the Ohlone Indian phrase for "the resting place of the hummingbird." It's what's left of this Almaden Air Force Station, a self-sustaining military community with 125 airmen and their families, constructed for our civil defense to make sure we weren't going to be invaded. That I was on a survey crew when the buildings were going up and did everything from putting stakes in the ground to using a tripod and transit makes it more personal. I remember it so well. The chief would pick me up, and it took us 45 minutes to get from Los Gatos and climb the unpaved, windy road to the top. They wanted to tear it down, and for many years, I've tried to help prevent that for history's sake. Today they knock down monuments left and right, but some things should be preserved to remind us and teach us, even though this tower has been exposed to the elements for six decades.

The base closed in 1980, and several years later, the open space district, a government agency, bought the property. All the accessory buildings were torn down, and the tower was going to be next. They basically didn't want to spend money to restore it. Thanks to many veterans and others who wanted to keep it up—including the Mount Umunhum Conservancy, a group dedicated to preserving the tower— the open district was pressed into changing plans and keeping it. Eventually, in 2016, it was deemed a historical landmark by the county, meaning it can't be demolished so long as it's cared for and in good shape, and a restoration plan was put in place before the pandemic.

It ultimately was turned into a public park for people to hike, bike, and ride horses, an 18,000-acre open preserve. Some people might say the tower isn't picturesque, but others would disagree, especially those who know its significance. More than that, this radar, with its spinning orange-and-white checkerboard antenna and 250-mile range, was part of history on another front. With the Air Force technicians and Department of Defense working with technological firms including IBM to modernize the radar program, it proved to be influential in the high-tech advancement and computer development that can be traced to the genesis of the Silicon Valley.

Chapter 50

Charity Begins at Home and Lasts Forever

PEOPLE ASK ME WHAT I'M MOST PROUD OF. I'm proud of my family. I'm proud of my children, my grandkids. I'm proud of the fact I was able to be successful. Now, there are many definitions of success. Does it mean becoming a millionaire? A billionaire? I define it as trying to be a good person, making a difference, and helping your fellow man. Defining success is hard to put your arms around. It's how you try to live your life. I don't ever want to live my life like I'm a big shot, but I feel very fortunate to be able to help organizations, schools, churches, and people from different backgrounds, whether they're in dire straits or trying to get help going to school.

"My oldest daughter is handicapped and was attending a special school in Millbrae. It's all privately funded, and they always struggled for funds. Steve and Pat sent the school money. They didn't ask anything but, 'Where do we send the check?' I always felt bad if people called Steve thrifty or a cheapskate. He will spend money if there's a good reason. All they wanted to know

was where to send the check. They didn't have to do that. When your employers do that, it endears you to them. We all want to be in a position to do something like that. There are a lot of people who can do it but don't. Believe me, I've flown them. Steve does."

—Mike Phillips, helicopter pilot

"We had the 60th reunion for our Santa Clara class of 1960 in 2021, a year later, because of the pandemic, and it was a wonderful time with a group of 70, including 43 of our alumni. It was held at the basketball court in the Schott Excellence Center, which is a beautiful facility. Well, Steve sponsored the whole dinner at $100 a plate, and he didn't want anyone to know. In the weeks before the reunion, one of the members of our class, Mel Russi, came up with some sort of strange disease affecting his heart, and doctors told him the only way to prolong his life was to take medication costing $19,000 a month. I called Steve to ask if he'd heard about Mel, and without as much as a New York nanosecond, Steve said, 'Tell him I'll pay for the medication.' Mel called me and cried when he heard from Steve. Ultimately Mel was able to get his insurance company to knock the price to $1,000 a month. The point is, that's who Steve is. I'm getting emotional telling this story."

—Butch Erbst, class of 1960

Sometimes it's about donating money, but it's also about encouraging others to reach their potential or at least reach a higher level, and that includes kids. I like the idea of helping kids further their opportunities in school, and one of my favorite programs when I was with the A's was Read to Succeed, which rewarded grade-school kids for reading books. Read an extra book, we'll get you tickets to an A's game. We partnered with Ken Leonard at Amdahl Corporation and used their corporate name to host an annual golf tournament featuring our A's players to raise money for Read to Succeed. Many times a school would take over an entire suite at the ballgame, and kids even got a chance to go to spring training, meet players, and get autographs. In fact, we eventually started running our own golf tournament through Citation Homes, mostly in San Mateo, which didn't involve players but homebuilders and subcontractors. We picked up all the expenses, and people would pay to play golf, and we'd raise all kinds of money to get kids into reading or encourage them to read more.

Donating to schools was always important to me, including Catholic schools, my roots. My grammar school, St. Clare's. My high school, Bellarmine. My college, Santa Clara. And the schools my kids went to, such as St. Francis High in Mountain View along with many others, including a somewhat new high school in Palm Desert, Xavier College Prep. Public schools too.

"Steve has given millions and millions of dollars to a lot of charities, more than $85 million in all. Much of it, the public doesn't know about. Early on, when I first started working with Steve, he came in my office and put a newspaper on my desk with an article about a family in the East Bay. There was a fire right before Christmas, and lives were lost. It was heartbreaking. Steve said he wanted to give money to this family and had me look into it. He didn't publicize it or want it publicized. He just wrote a check. After 9/11, he came in my office and said he wanted to give money to the firefighters back in New York, so we sent a check. He does a lot of things unsolicited, and he loves to give money to things he believes in, such as schools and hospitals. Those are areas in which he believes he can make a difference. Constantly giving is something that's ingrained in his lifestyle.

"He doesn't spend money needlessly. He doesn't throw money around or do crazy things like buy yachts. Driving around

in his 1999 Mercedes kind of epitomizes Steve. He doesn't need all the flash and prestige of a new car. He doesn't need all those electronics and computer chips. He'll take the push-button radio. He wants to get where he wants to go as easily and efficiently as he can. It kind of summarizes his life and, to me, his business. He's results-oriented, very practical. The same guy he always was, and he thinks there's more value in putting back into society."

—Dan Ikeda, chief financial officer,
SCS Development Company

When I give to organizations, they like to acknowledge me. But that's not why I do it. I do it because it's right, because it's necessary, because it brings smiles to faces. When I give to individuals, I don't want my name to be known. Sometimes you can't help it. I think it's important to get more people involved, encourage others to chip in so that it's more of a collaborative effort, more people feeling proud about contributing. I'll do that a lot, donate a sum and ask others to match it.

I started giving money away way back when I was poor. I always tried to give something, 100 bucks here, 200 bucks there. If I felt good about the charity, if something was close to my heart, I really couldn't say no. That's still the case. Some donations are up front, some become long-term commitments. It doesn't matter if you come from humble beginnings, like I did, or if you inherit a fortune. If you have it, you should give it away. I wanted to make a lot of money, and I did all that, but what good is that in the end? I could spend money all day. I'd rather give it to charity and to people who need it more. That's what I enjoy. Now that's a thrill.

Acknowledgments

I WISH TO EXPRESS MY SINCERE THANKS to those who helped with this book and supported me throughout the process and throughout my life, including my family, friends, and work associates.

I'd like to acknowledge some people who aren't mentioned in the book, including two mentors from Santa Clara University. One is Charles Dirksen, the dean of the business school who looked out for me and helped me get my first job at Ford Motor Company. When my grades slipped, he gave me nice warnings to work harder. Another is Father Bart O'Neill, a theology professor who was my guardian angel, counselor, and confidant. He looked out for me and knew more about me than I knew about myself.

Also, two close friends from the university: Pat Carroll, who became a stockbroker and financial adviser, and Dennis McGrath, who played ball with me in college and became an Oakland policeman and later went into private investigation.

From Bellarmine College Prep in San Jose, I'd like to recognize Jim Mieuli, who has organized our regular luncheons (the second Tuesday of every month) for members of the class of 1956, a great opportunity to keep in contact with our classmates and friends.

I've been fortunate to work with many talented people in the business world, including Peter Au, my right-hand man for three decades until he retired in 2014. I had a huge trust in Peter. He knew me as well as anybody, a very smart guy with a knack and nose for real estate who thought outside the box when crunching numbers and advising me on projects, including a successful property right across from the old Apple headquarters in Cupertino that he negotiated for us and another one near the mall in Newark that we purchased and eventually turned around for a nice profit. Without Peter, I'm sure we wouldn't have done so many deals or been so successful.

Dan Ikeda, who worked under Peter and replaced him as CFO, has been very helpful and loyal to me as a smart, all-around good guy who gives me a lot of advice and is very sharp with analysis. Ken Perry, who started out as a purchasing agent, worked his way to vice president of construction and does a superb job. We wouldn't be where we are without him. Janet Bowers, our executive assistant, has been instrumental with the daily undertakings at our company and a huge help on many fronts in putting together this book. I'd be lost without her.

Sadly, we lost Sam Spear before this project's completion. Sam greatly assisted me when I owned the A's, and we remained very close. He was a major inspiration in setting this book in motion, connecting me with John Shea, and advising every step of the way.

A special thanks to Paul DePodesta, the former Oakland A's assistant general manager who was kind enough to write a terrific and candid foreword. I always thought highly of Paul and knew he would be successful because he had all the characteristics for success. I wish him the best in his current role with the Cleveland Browns and hope he wins a Super Bowl.

I'd also like to thank photo editor Brad Mangin, index editor Kurt Aguilar, and Triumph editor Michelle Bruton, along with Deanne Fitzmaurice, the Pulitzer Prize–winning photographer who took the shot on the book's cover.

I have warmth in my heart for St. Simon Church and the congregation members at our 6:30 AM mass, including Mary Baumel, Jerry Buckley, Raymond Burkley, Arthur Carmichael, Bernice Comfort, Jerome Crowley, Ed and Donna Daly, Pat Deppmeier, Joe and Maria Gallo, Judy Howard, Bernie and Marian Marren, Margaret McCarthy, Tim McClenahan, Peter Pazmany, Jean Rousseau, Melvin Russi, Lou Ryan, my sister-in-law Joanne Schott, Phil Sheridan, Ben Stetson, and Patricia Sweeney.

Lastly, I wanted to mention a wonderful group at the Wynn Hotel in Las Vegas, where Pat and I visit, nice people who work in the tower café and have become my friends: Justin, Saul, Sabrina, and Emely.

Sources

Page 4: Mary Schott, *Saratoga News*, January 22, 2003. 7: Edgar Schott, career summary from the first registered engineer in the city of Santa Clara, from 1940 until 1969. 12 and 13: Stephen DeArmond, *Journal of Neuropathology & Experimental Neurology*, June 13, 2017. 71: George Vukasin, *San Francisco Chronicle*, May 20, 1992. 146–47: Wally Haas, *San Francisco Chronicle*, June 14, 2009.

Index